"Just Writing"

Book One: Transcending

"Just Writing"

Book One: Transcending

By: April Love

© 2020, Just Writing, Book One: Transcending
By: April Love- All Rights Reserved
Published by: A Love Writing

All rights reserved. No part of this book may be reproduced in any form on by an electronic or mechanical means, including information storage and retrieval systems, without permission in writing from the publisher, except by a reviewer who may quote brief passages in a review.

Cover Image/Design: Shirley Pendarvis- (Visual Effects)
Printed in the U.S.A
ISBN: 978-0-578-70094-6 (Print)
To contact me send an email to alovedivinity2020@gmail.com.

"From the heart, the mind, and the soul...
The written word have the ability to express them all."

~April Love

Dedication

This book is dedicated to the people who have the thoughts, the feelings, and the emotions- but don't have the words to express them...

Acknowledgments

Life
Love
Light

Foreword

"Just Writing" is titled from the constant saying of "I'm just writing" when asked what I was doing as people ALWAYS saw me with pencil and paper. I seemed like a "brain" to some, as they would shake their head and say "whatever". Little did they know I was "escaping" and writing about love, life and the difference between the dark and light of the human experience. Of course all there is between- in which I either witnessed or experienced. But more importantly... about the creation and/or destruction of a soul- as you will read.

Being, living and working in a world where people are constantly at war between the dark and light, begs the question "why?"... "what is that?"... and why do some fare well and others don't? But no matter the circumstances... own it, honor it and transcend above it.

That's what I was doing 'just writing." Letting it all go into a sea of letters that washed away all the defeat yet restored my greatness and gave me the freedom necessary to achieve my goals.

Contents

Intro...	iv
Love's POV	1
Love's Quest	2
Spirit Soul Life	16
Black Radiance	38
Frantic Reality	51
Love Lust and Longing	71
Letters to My Love	94
Seeds of Life- the Children	110
Transcending	120
Favorite Quotes and Sayings	146
About the Author	152

Intro...

What you hold in your hand is my essence-

The writings in this book come from the very deepest part of me; inspired by life, living, and love. It's the very core of me to express to you my creativity and love for the written word. With that, I am grateful for those who have acquired this book and given me a chance to connect with you in ways that only words can do. So without further ado, here I am, "Just Writing"...

Love's POV

Remember Love

Remember Love, if nothing else
Remember what it means
Remember where it comes from
Remember what it brings

Remember how to feel it
Remember how to show it
Remember that it's in your heart
Where the Creator wants you to hold it

To my family- "You", I pray-
I pray love carries you, through the day
I pray you see, your beauty inside
I pray no matter what, you express it in life

I know the world is crazy and mad
I know others make you feel bad and sad
I know you wish they'd understand
And take the time to hold your hand

Know it's not you, it's them
And it's not them, it's you
I pray that love with grace and mercy
Will always get you through

Remember this... if nothing else
The love
The life
The light....
That lives inside the self

Love's Quest

Love's Gift

Love is a natural gift of life
Bred by the Creator, as all things...
An emotion that can bring joy
And emote pain
It's peculiar, familiar, and similar to
Everything we know and want to attain

It feels good, bad, happy, and sad
Makes you laugh and cry, live and die
It can be real, phony, mad, and sound
Make you shout out, "Thank you, God!"
Or cry out "God, why!"

Love is what we know from birth
Into a family, into life
It's everywhere, somewhere, all the time
Causing happiness and security- putting the heart at ease
Causing grief and pain- putting it to shame

Love has no beginning and no end
It's passed and surpassed
Alive in the living and remembered in the dead
Heals all things- yet complex in truth
And when you don't know what tomorrow may bring...
It doesn't matter... because with love...
Every day is brand new

What's Love

Love is the most complex, complicating, confusing thing: inside your nerves are on end, your heart races, and your soul sings. Repeatedly, it's no wonder that love has its means: the means to allow you to breathe in loving.

So hard to get, when you get it, it's good. But when the flip side of it goes down- love is crude. Not really, but with your emotions- you gotta get control, because love can make you lose your mind- your heart on hold- actions that can destroy your soul- all because you lost self-control.

Everyone wants to feel it, see it, hear it, touch it, and taste it.
Want to know it, show it, give it, live it, and be it.
Love.
If it was that easy, we would be the picturesque of happiness in the creator's eyes- with love to guide, and love to follow, love in our vision, love in our eyes...
Loving
Living
Life
The reasons why we were created... Love... it is the Soul's Light

Love Recognition

You know how we sometimes wonder about that word Love
Love
We know that it's the most prized reward to have
The notice of humanity by who we are- what we do
Love
The four-letter word we use to let people know they are that important, special one
Love
A word that's taken for granted
A feeling that isn't a feeling
Love
The 21st century... in the face of a new era
The love you know is BULLSHIT
And no longer exist

I AM LOVE

DaDeepestLove- Part 1

However I may be— I am who I am
The one you love to hate
But don't mistake
Only those who have an open mind
Can look into the truth of L-O-V-E
And see the meaning of my existence
In a world that makes us scream

I shine in the eyes of happiness
But am constantly haunted by greed and selfishness
To have me is a burden
A weight on your mind, a strain on your heart
What I am is a spirit, alive and known
I go from here to there and am everywhere
And everywhere I go, I grow
But the darkness behind me,
Scars everything I've been in and known

It's not so easy to be me
Though I am beautiful, a part of fantasies and dreams
I get dissed and dismissed because of ignorance
And those close-minded or either foolish
And out for sexual bliss

I know that I am scary...
Hard to contain
Hard to understand
Hard to maintain

I get used and abused
From those who have crude and tasteless attitudes
Want me for what they want
Need me for what I can do
Use me for what they can obtain
Throw me away when they have all they wished to gain

I am Love
Beautiful in name, talented in the mind
Deep within hearts, and known by all
I am a fighter, a winner, an essence full of emotion
I am intimidating, wonderful, comfortable, and true

However I may be, I am who I am.
Though my name is misused, trashed, used, and bashed
I am still within the Heart, Mind, Spirit, and Soul
I am DaDeepestLove

DaDeepestLove- Part 2

However I may be- I am who I am...
Love
DaDeepestLove

Don't be surprised about what's within my eyes
You wouldn't want to see- not even a peek
I won't lie. But I won't tell
All I know is the Devil has cast a spell
I feel confused, and torn, in pain, and want to be reborn
But I've lived the life of a hundred lives
And one day I'm scared to wake up and hear that I died

So I try inside- to live out life
Have slowed down and sacrificed... but in mind-
I'm still not all right
So what am I to do? Stay faithful and true?
And give myself only to me?
But how can that be when I know I'm the love we need

I'm trying to get it right with the children:
I want them to know love and happiness-
Not misuse, abuse, and hiding the truth
I want them to be free to live a better reality
Not always hard times and crawling to catch their dreams
I want them to be the blessed with a good home, good mom and good dad
Family to help them stay strong,
And not let them stray, trying to find love on their own

I'm DaDeepestLove!
A love that need love, give love, is love, and true in love
A man, a woman, a child, a team...
A struggle of hatred- trying to be redeemed
How can I stand for something, if I'm being fallen for everything?

Someone, help me- help me please!
I'm here crying for forgiveness on bended knees
Crying for savior on bended knees
Crying to live till I'm eons old
Divine recreation of my spirit, heart, and soul

I don't want to keep going around blind,

Trying to find,
A heart to be found
When all I hear is the sounds of my tears flowing down

What do I do? I'm trying to get through,
But I can't seem to cope,
I'm feeling high and feeling broke
No joke- this new world must be a hoax
'Cause it's just not fair that some die young
While others live and live.
I'm not too alive- not too dead
What is that I really am?

Struggling to evolve into something more,
Something beautiful,
Something sure,
Something better than I've ever been before
DaDeepestLove-
That's for sho.

Fuck Love

I am Love-
Love that no more exist
The love people yearn for
But know not what it mean
I can't be figured out-
I'm hard to contain-
The way I feel,
It's hard to explain
As real as I am-
I'm used in vain

Love- unnoticed in reality
I hate that I have to live upon others formalities
It's hard being me- I'm the one who endures all the pain
A storm I remain- ones that come and go
Mother Nature is not at work with what storms I've known

Inflicted upon me is a world of insanity,
Heartlessness and ignorance
My heart, so open
It's hard to be amongst others who's isn't
So I try to be shitty and closed off too
The kind of love that turncoat, leaving people sad and blue

But I am Love-
You see it on TV-
But TV can't even depict the love we want to achieve
Maybe the next lifetime, what we see will be how we be
What we need is to rewind in time, then press play again

Fuck Love- a lot- most people say
Is it so much hatred that the hearts' gone astray
How did that come to be?
We all know that love is what we need-

So here I am-
I am Love
"Fuck Love" your attitude say-
A beautiful thought, none-the-less
Yet not around much these days
So if "Fuck Love" is the mentality of the world today,
Why not we all just say "Fuck off and Have a hateful day"

Real Love Is

Real Love is a part of life-
The gift of the Creator- the gift that is light
Without it evil will condemn the soul

Real Love is a notice of humility and emotional stability
Real Love exists in the spirit, conscious, and physical form
Real Love is out of this world-
A destination unknown

Without Love we wouldn't be
Love is why we breathe
Love is the means of reproduction, life, and unity

Real Love is to be loved
Real Love is to be given completely
Real Love is to be true-
That there is a care in the world about SOMEONE/THING
Real Love is given and taken equally-
Should not have to play for, work for, or pray for

Real Love is the truth that lies in you
When there is Real Love within you,
You will know that it's real
And the realness is truth

Where Love Resides

There comes a time
When love settles us down
As crazy as the world seems
Nothing can make you totally unhappy

When you stare into a child's eyes
When you write love letters telling why
When you just "be" with love
It's so simple to show what's in your heart

In the heart- resides the love we want and need
What shows our feelings and humanity
Where the light of the soul comes from
To recognize that the Creator is a part of us
To give off love that only "It" would want to bring
To show affection every heart desires makes it sing
Love

How else can we flush out hate?
The darkness of emotions
The killer of the souls

Show what's in the heart...
Where love resides

Those Who Love

From the sky to the waters, as all hearts come together
The people who give freely
Are those who love

A voice as a harp
A soft kiss as a feather
People who care for all
Are those who love

Sometimes I wonder how life would be
If there was no poverty, pain, or defeat
The only ones who will make that change so everyone can be free
Are those who love

Love Obsession

Love Obsession
Obsession of the mind, body, and soul
To feel and connect with "one"
Kindred Spirits, united in love

Obsessed with the thought
The magnitude of a feeling that's an outer-body experience
More of a high than any drug can seize
Love Obsession

To feel so complete
To feel like not only your organism connect
But...
In Your spirit, Your heart- soul

Setting a communion for everlasting and everlasting

Obsessed with love
To be fulfilled and given, toyed and moved into space
Through the grounds of the heart's desire
Burning flames from what the soul inspires

Love Obsession
As we go on and live through our daily routines
We who don't possess love...
Are obsessed with the makings love can bring

When Love Isn't Enough

When love isn't enough
But all you want to feel
What do you do to make it work?
You know... to keep it real

When love isn't enough
Who's really to blame?
Shattered pieces of your heart
Feeling all ashamed

Ashamed of the rights and wrongs
The fights that lasted all night long
Tears smearing your vision
Not the way to feel
Moments you cry inside
For when love made you heal

When love isn't enough
What do you do?
How do you remember?
That love is within you

How can you forget that it started with love?
The light from the Creator- sent with love
All you need and wanted in life
Had it strong- giving you life

Eventually pain- a permanent stain
Who's to blame- who's at fault
When fear of the end coming, begins to stalk
Your mind, your heart, your body disowned

When love isn't enough
Is it right or wrong?

Never Give Up on Love

TV depicts the fantasy of love
Family depicts the sharing needs of love
Friendship depicts the common needs of love
Romance depicts the desired need of love

You think it'll never be for you
You don't believe in the certainty of what it can do
People mock and let you down and try to break you
Regardless... never give up on love

You try to provide what's missing inside
You send your Heart, Mind, Body and Soul
Through tremors that eat you alive
Your emotion, beliefs, trust, and all that should have been
Got exchanged and rearranged; dismayed, and delayed
Never being what they seemed and needed to be
To help you hold on to your dreams

Regardless... never give up on love

When Will We Have Love

I'm happy with my accomplishments
But not happy with myself
When will I accomplish love?
Love I need from someone else
Am I not as wonderful as-
The beach house I wish to own
Overlooking an ocean or sea

I feel I am all of that
And sunshine
Lightly touching a face
When will I have love from another?
And not feel so displaced

True it may be- all we need is self-love
To make us whole inside
Emotionally, without it being shared
Begins to tear up the emotional pride

Mistakes we made to feel the love
And love a love from our fantasy
We don't know what the Creator has in store
But the void keeps it a dream

So when will we have love from another?
To obtain love for ourselves as a whole
And give to the world the love within
The love that light up our soul

Spirit Soul Life

The Metamorphosis

When I look into the mirror, exactly what do I see?
Sometimes I see me now, sometimes the true me
Whatever the reason, I feel I am in someone else
What lies deep inside and underneath is that of someone else
Truly its destiny, the me I truly see

When it comes to the truth of it all
I really need to be real about who I am
For what lies beneath is a woman-
A queen of the world that is in me
So when I look in the mirror I see...

The metamorphosis of... Love

The Metamorphosis- "L"

Looking at Life
Looking at Love
Looking at Living- the life I dream of
Looking to see that all can come true
Living my life in prosperity, to bloom
Looking at me, I see I'm still young
Older in age- enough to grow up
Love is me, although loving me is hard
Why must I learn, to love me as God

I know who I am
I know the real me
Looking into my soul, I'm confused by what I see
Worthy of the silver, of the platinum, of the gold
Love- overall- is what I should behold

Looking at Life
Looking at Love
Looking at Living- the life I dreamed of
Success, Perseverance, Educated, Bank Accounts with six z's
Mirrored images of the magazines, TV, music, and movies
Loving children, loving husband- loving family
Picture-perfect, close to miraculous- the life that's for me

Looking at reality, it's hard- but can be achieved
Looking at how hard I work, I know it's in me
Looking at the way I've changed, I know it's ahead
Life, Love, and Living is for sure inside of "L"

The Metamorphosis- "O"

"Over with" is all I can feel
Other than the love inside- trying to overspill
Some days I'm overkill with emotion- overall in doubt
Am I the only one to feel this way?
Or is what's inside going to fail
Am I going to feel this wholeness in me?
Or always angry, feeling defeat

One thing I know is the "O" in love is one and overall-
The circle of a life- the completeness of a soul
Inside and out, beauty isn't doubt
We all have the infinite possibilities
To live on and throughout
Overall I am one that love lives throughout-
Because I have, visions of dreams
Visions of all the things I can achieve
Visions of completeness, feeling L-O-V-E

The Metamorphosis- "V"

Visions of Love
Visions of Life
Visions of Greatness
Visions of Light

Be amazed by what you can do
Be not afraid of what you can prove
Those who don't see, can not conceive
The notion of truth, the truth in belief

Believe in yourself
Be a visionary
Vision yourself with love
Happy and merry

Visions of bliss
With the creator- you exist
To be one with self-
Inside your metamorphosis

The Metamorphosis- "E"

Evolution...
Evolving to the end
To begin again
To recreate life again

The metamorphosis of the soul
To become whole
The evolution of your consciousness
Knowing what you behold

Never underestimate your truth
Never minimize your life
Always inner-stand your plight
To morph into light

Everyone, everywhere
Listen with your heart
Know that your fears is not as they seem
But forces evolving, in what you perceive

Even your dreams evolves what you believe
Your subconscious mind- planting the seed
Love evolves the things, you should aim to achieve
And light your soul with the metamorphosis of
L.O.V.E.

Believe in "You"

When life seems to fail you
Do you know what failure means?
To win in life, there has to be
A dream that manifest a dream

When you awaken to the darkness
When your soul is flooded in black
Do you dare to try and love?
Or are afraid and hold love back

How do you conquer life?
How do you conquer fear?
How do you build the confidence?
To live beyond the tears

When love and dreams stay on your mind
And the will to be happy stays in your heart
Do you ever wonder one step is all it takes
To start from where you stopped

A dreamer dreams but never "do"
Flowers grow and sunshine bloom
Lovers love, when love is true
A dream in love, can come true

Are you a failure?
A winner or beginner
Do your try hard to knock down walls
Or do you walk away a quitter

Sometimes you have to fight
A good fight doesn't kill
When you get back up and live again
Then you know your will

Failures are quitters
Dreamers never do
To win and make your dreams come true
You have to start believing in "You"

Alone

Alone
A fetus in the womb
Striving for life, air- to be set free
No one around- just you

Like being connected to the cord
Yet you want to be living off the cord of life
Your own life
Alone

But how do you know if it's the beginning or the end
Look around at your accomplishments
Within the world you're known to be in
Alone

Do you fear the threat of reality?
Feeling like you can't do it by yourself
But you get through beautifully
Alone

Taking time out to plan your strategy
And be prosperous in the way you seek
You must take time to be...
Alone

Quietness

Peace have yet settled in the room
Unto I think this joy of quietness will ever last

Oh, the annoying noises I've heard before
Now carried away as someone shuts the door
Enveloped in a hollow space with quietness

As noise fades away in the distance
All the thoughts of nothing to clear your head will come in
You will soon fell how good it is when quietness is around

Happy you will be that all loudness is gone
Able to get your head together all alone
Then you will appreciate the goodness of quietness

Emotions

Feeling it in your pit
The desire for something real
The longing of something near
Yet far

Containing your fury
The hurt that's filled inside
Letting go-
That's hard

Emotions is what they are

Peace in Mind

When I pour out my heart
In a wail of tears
I stain my soul
With unforeseen fears

I wipe my face
With the back of my hand
And wonder how to start over-
How to began

Seeing my face
Withered and frowning
Want much more than anything
To keep from drowning

As sleep preys
Upon my troubled mind
I ask for dreams
That can stop my cries

How High

When I think back, I wonder what made me fall prey to the bud
They say bud is a drug- I say like "whoa!"
Shit, I was high as the fucking moon and stars-
What the fuck- smoke all the pain away
Sex, bud, partying- my pleasure, what's your desire?
To think of who it was, when it was, and how it was...
Sometimes all in a cloud of smoke- But not really

Accomplishing life is hard enough to do
I wish I started back when skies were crystal clear and blue
Not smoggy, full of the smoke
That I thought the high would lift me up to
On those days and nights I used to love being high-
Looking up at the sky where my mind was further above
Zoned out

Trying to stay up is so hard
When something always trying to knock you down
Or make you weak
I find myself feeling depressed and looking sad-
Wanting to stay upbeat- feel free
So I get the urge sometimes to obtain my old friend-
Mr. Green

I have a child, and you know they be in some shit
Got to be where she is...
But the high won't take me from the place where I sit-
But my goals for her and I lye where:
High society- educated with degrees- 6-z bank accounts-
Stocks growing like the life of me

Life is hard, but living is beautiful
Nothing to be seen as a reappearing miracle
What would happen if we don't see our children through?
They'd be shit on a stick from the neglect we inflict-
Spoiled, unruly, and so more like us
We must be a good example to make them a better us

So here I come world, open your arms to me
I'd give my all, my heart, my mind, my love
Just for you to see-
I want to live, succeed and give
And go back to where I belong...
the Ultimate High

Underneath/Within

Underneath it all
Within times of affliction
My body yearns to be withheld
From life's worldly deception

Have I not answers to my questions
Have I not been through enough pain
Have I not enough nightmares
Have I not the time to heal

Underneath the mask, within my soul
Love beholds, but the cruelty of love
Stains my soul
Why let love be exposed

Granted is what I wish not
What I wish not, is what I see
Leveled down within myself
The agony of life's defeat

Thrashing in my heart a need
Underneath the terror of it all
When I wake up to see the sun so bright
I go to sleep underneath sight

Listen to me, the world is madd
Insane I see as children are dead
Insane I see as war shed blood
Listen to me, the time will come

As the races of blood underneath
So much the same
As the crowdedness of emotion
A butterfly slain

Love, underneath
Heart, within
Soul transpires
To restore love inside sin

Why

Why, I ask God
Why is it I'm last?
Why is it I'm not worthy of obtaining it all
Why do I still lie in wait?

I seem to have so many obstacles that stand in my way
Like a rat race and 100 million dollars
But love is my wealth
I can't seem to go the longer stretch of it
Just halfway through before the car breaks down
The driver leaves me in the desert
Or my plane crash and I'm airborne and falling- alone
Why?

Is it because I haven't finished loving or accepting myself
And/or changing the flaws of my image
Maybe the mental thoughts of the past
Or opened my heart, with its built up emotion
At last

I find out and see that it's always a replay of history
A little different in content- but the same ending
I mean what, why, when can I expect
Can someone hear me, feel me
You know what I've gone through to desperately seek thee

I see that I first had to start with me
Loving myself, like every breath I breathe
Given by love
And every day I see, but...
Why, oh, why?
Why am I so lonely?
Why do I feel like I'm in a world where it's only me?

My Life

Every time I try to do right
It ends up being wrong
I try to understand myself and help people understand me
No matter what happens, the right never seems to be

Some say I'm not mature
I need to grow up and be responsible
They don't know I try
I do what I can
They make me feel like nothing
Like that's who I am

My self-esteem is low- it needs to be boosted
So I can let myself go and get loosened
Do things like them
And maybe be a clone
Be miserable and unhappy- is that what they want

Under all the fakeness, there's me
Someone who is immature and lacking responsibility
I know I'm getting older and I know what to do
But only to myself, I have something to prove
And take charge of my life- it's my life

Stormy Waters of Life

Sometimes, most of the time, you feel knocked down. Waves crashing into you bring you towards darkness and far from light. You're searching for where land begins but you feel it's nowhere near.

Darkness in your emotions and your mental state is distraught- your soul out of light. Stormy waters of your mischief wrong doings pulling you into the darkness from sight.

Inspiring a tune of letting go, but can't find the strength to do so; letting go is hard, holding on is worst to do. Knocking you down and pulling you out, as the waves wash the fears running through. Looking back at what's left behind, trying to catch your breath as you sink into the deep unknow- sinking into a darkness that's your soul.

Stormy waters come and go, up to you how to flow, nice and smooth or rough as hell. It's ok just don't let go, get the strength to swim ashore. Don't play in darkness anymore, because these stormy waters of life may grasp your soul.

Strangers

You know, you never really know someone. When you think you do, all of a sudden, the stranger inside comes through. You tell your secrets, share your pain and joy; the love inside makes you damn near show your soul.

The people you see, going through strife, the friend you've known most of your life, the partner you've seek that make your toes curl, goes in and out of who they are every time they step into the world.

Don't think you know someone- because you don't. When the stranger comes out its usually taunt; hurt up torn up lit up, pissed off; how can the one you love do this to you. Become something else and make you feel like a fool. Don't get caught up in the illusion, its confusion. The fusion of the other personality.

But also know there's a stranger in you....
We are even strangers to ourselves- so watch what you do...

Clean Slate

What will it take
To have a clean slate
To start all over again
And not feel gutted from within

What does it take
To pay all the debts
To pay the rent for a year
To sit at home with a blunt and a beer

What does it take
To fix your love life
To lose the weight and keep it off
To not want to fight

What should you do
When people igg you
When people make you cuss
When they make you wanna fuck shit up

What should you do
To feel good about you
To feel confident through and through
And not be afraid to be the real you

What do you say
When people get in your way
When your dreams are stunted
And you can't move your issues out the way

To be free is hard
To hold on is shit
To not be able to let go-
'Cause super glue makes you stick

A clean slate- what does it take?

Destiny

In my mind I see these things
Things I feel are a part of my destiny
It is not fantasy, imagination, illusion
My life I want it not to be a delusion

I want a house on the beach where sand castles can be made
On the rocks, near the Ocean or Sea are yet my peaceful remedies
To say I'll never have, is a faith yet lost
To say I will, is a challenge I'll take head on

My life is a movie, a novel, a song, a play
My life is imagination, fantasy, dreams, and reality
For what I have now truly come to believe
Is my spirit and soul lead me towards my destiny

My mind is the beginning
My heart is the call
My legs help me stand up to
My feet carry me on

I listen to my gut and inner voice
For that's the Creator speaking within me
Only saying things
That'll lead me to the becoming of my destiny

As I set forth and face reality
I strengthen my being as I move forward
To create my reality
Not my fantasies or dreams- but my Destiny

Better Life

Sometimes I wonder if everything would be alright
Living in a world where no one kill, curse, or fight
Or disrespect life so easily
Everybody loving everything, exceptionally

Sure enough our world is going to end
It's our fault that we can't fight to truly live
To make a better place for our kids
Teach them love and respect...
But it's hard when all we do is praise sin
We see in their eyes the confusion that lies
And say "be good"   as we kill each other
And cause our demise

Take care of them- show them the way
So our next generation of youngsters won't go astray
Tell them to always keep love in their heart
Truth in their mind-
Belief in self, is a good start
Be a good example to the child and all of the time
So it can be a better place for us, to have a better life
Next time around

Looking at my Life

Looking at my life I see:
Hard times and good times
Those to learn from and appreciate
Given by all triumphs-
I learned to succeed, push through, and stand
Stand on two feet- feet that are my own
Life itself has done no wrong
Looking at the mistakes, the rewards,
The knowledge I have consumed within- by living

Looking at my life I see:
My children:
Conceived by me, grew within me, birthed by me, raised by me
My shadow that lingers
My blood that flows to my heart- the image of myself
A Blessing
Nothing I can do in my life without their presence
I must live, breath, sacrifice, and improve for them
They depend on me to show them the way

Looking at my life I see:
I must work for what I want
Supply myself what I need
And push through what holds me back
I must sacrifice to get the truer things that mean most
I must be independent and focus on my dependents

Looking at my life I see... what life truly means

I've Decided...

I've decided...
To not be so selfish and self-absorbed or blaming of others
I'm a grown ass woman, who has her own mind, her own bills, her own life- And responsibilities
I will, can, and am in control
I'm the director and star in my life
My vision is my destiny
My dreams, goals, and visions won't cease as long as I remain in the light...

I've decided...
No more games, lies, self-destruction.
No more heartbreak that shouldn't and didn't have to be.
No more bullshit from the lips of creeps.
No more free ass, no more on bended knees.
No more following, for I am in the lead.
No more worries, pain, or distress.
No more worrying about what's left for the universe to handle of the mess.
No more crying, no more tear stains.
No more staring at a soul deprived of love without restraint.

I've decided...

To Live

Questions in Life

Why is it hard?
Why do bad things happen to good people?
When will the deservers of love receive?
When will a sick child or adult get the cure they need?
When will a mother or father get their shit together to provide for their future?
When will a man get off the nipple of another mother?
When will a woman save herself for a real man?
When will I have love, happiness, stability, and peace?
When will I ever be assured that my child and I will live out our dreams?
When will I ever get saved?
Will it be soon?
When will I ever make Love to _____ under the moon?
Will I be rich, stay struggling, be poor?
When will I return, back to the unknown?

Black Radiance

The Power of Being Black

It's a powerful thing being black these days
Others seem, to follow our ways
Always a revolution
Even when they try to stop our fusion

In so many ways we can bring each other up
And knock ourselves straight down
We can drag each other through the mud
Then wash us in the crowds

I love that we're so inventive
How we take nothing and make it everything
But with that come responsibility
And that's looking out for all of "we"

I tell myself that when I have enough money
I'm starting a foundation to raise our people up
I know that it takes power, dedication and strength
Because money isn't always enough

The power of being black is how we strive
Although we struggle just to stay alive
So why turn our nose up and look down on our own
When slave masters and sellouts had us dishonor our throne

When all other groups
Have a stake and common goal
They pursue it together
And look out for their own

With the power we have to unify all others
It doesn't make sense why we can't love each other
The power is infamous and should be used for a greater good
For the power of our blackness is what they use

The Black Woman

Don't you love how a black woman struts: the swing of her hips and the jiggle of her butt; a form-fitting outfit she wears to perfection- a shade that goes with attitude, feeling, and even her complexion; looking so good your eyes can't seem to wander from- for the black woman you see, her aura is a mystery

Naturally nappy, cropped or dread- shaved or cut off, a bald sexy head; tracks and braids, individuals and styles out the ass; I'm talking about a sophisticated lady- not one who is of ghetto trash

Sexy as shit is she, with her manicure, designed nails and toes; a real woman that's not afraid, to let the blemishes show; full lips, pretty smile, and an exquisite black nose; arresting eyes with deepness and knowledge inside- she has charisma, beauty and individual style

Single mother or wife, deepens her love for her family and self; but as she comes more on her own and take care of her own, she grows so much in mind that when it comes to nonsense she explodes- so please know

Goal-oriented and ambitious- a true queen of a woman in the making; a great friend, a real mother, a faithful sister, daughter, wife and lover; she knows about life through experience and wisdom given by all; gets up and press on when life makes her fall; don't let stress kill her spirit, because it's all gone be alright; work through all the pain to get to the glory of love and living a good life

A black woman knows about struggle, and still makes it by any means necessary; it's in our heart to work it out and get through; it's a part of a Black Woman's HerStory

The Black Man

Chocolate, sexy as hell, melaninated head to toe; deep dark eyes, full tasty lips, and that big sexy nose; that thing that hangs between his legs- blacker the berry, sweeter the juice- any of you who've met him before know the saying is usually true

Features and characteristics like no other man- can't be broken in this here land; been through hell and back again, but has enough courage to fight to live; I'm not talking strictly about the ghetto thug- I'm talking about the good black men we love

He has gone through mess but kept straight up... now he's managing programs in his community club; the leaders, producers, directors, entrepreneurs, mentors, and educators who are on the scene. Raising us up and doing right. Surely he's a king.

The family man, the care giver, the woman lover- the love within him; the not so typical one you know; the one that hates to be stereo-typed, knowing that he takes his kids to school and tucks them in bed at night

The one who has put the past behind; the one who's not afraid to grow in his mind; the one who expresses his feelings inside; and the scarce ones who admits he's f'd up and won't lie; the one who knows right from wrong; the one who takes a beating and stay strong; the one who knows that violence is not the way, and adjust to the way the world is today

The one who looks in the mirror and sees a good man- a man that can make it in the white man's land; a man who has respect and tries not to disrespect or neglect what makes him that man

He's a lover, a father, a husband, a brother, a son; he's a business man, a strong man, a powerful man, a good man, a real man; he's the Black Man.

All I Want is Chocolate

Oh my chocolate soldier- sweet and plentiful
Dark and handsome is what you are
The presence of you begging me to enjoy you completely
Wisp me away to Candy Land-
You're like a 3 Musketeers I craves to have
Full of chocolaty pleasure
I close my eyes, kiss your lips and taste your nougat and treasures

You melt in my mouth as I savor you with my hands
As I endure every bit of you, my mind is in Candy Land
Thinking of gumdrops, lollipops, s'moores
Taking me to my peak, making me so weak

Bad as it may be, damn it's so good
Because it's the deserting pleasure I need
You are the very bitter and sweet:
Brownie, cookie, candy bar
And all other succulent treats

You are in all, my chocolate heaven-
The one I take to sleep
The yearning I feel makes me need it all the more
And all I can say is... all I am, and all I want, is chocolate

My Sistah

The only person available at 2am
The only person that'll hear me out when my nerves are on end
The only one who got my back if shit is to go down
The only one who accepts me- even if I'm not wearing a diva crown

My sistah, is my P.I.C., my confidant and forever friend
She boosts me up when I'm feeling low, or put her two cents in it
She understands who I am, and why I feel the way I feel
She's the truest confidant I got- and we always keep it real

From back in the day, till today, we always had a connection
Never could we stray too far apart-
Without rebounding the interception
No matter what, we're together, and even my man must know-
Me and him is each other's life- but me and her still gone roll

Good and Bad, Right and Wrong, Thick and Thin, We Are Strong
Years and years, and we still counting- what she means is a lot to me
Ladies, if you have a real friend- please respect them- really
'Cause no matter who walks out, or turns away
Your sistah is the person who loves you for you, and is there to stay

Catfish, Collard Greens, & Good Ole Pork N Beans

I remember being in the kitchen, opening the pots
Simmering inside was something good and hot
Damn those days seem present to me
Dripping from my chin, the juice of collard greens

Picked from the fields; I helped them get clean
They were stankin' so good- like daddy's feet
Never mind that, give me a bowl- and fill it up-
And once the beans and fish done, put that in front

Ah, fishing! Those days on the bay-
Grabbing up the pole, excited about the meal ahead
Trying to catch the biggest one,
"Oh damn. I think I got it!"
Dad came over and helped me out (That was a special moment)

Took them home in an old paint bucket-
That had seen many days and fish
Spread out the newspaper and laid them out
While mama scaled them clean

Simmering in the old iron skillet
The smell filling the air
In 15 minutes they were done
And I was already ready

Pork-N-Beans, what can I say-
The food that stands for survival
But cousin made them up real sweet
And added butter so rich to me

Soon I was sittin' with catfish, collard greens,
And some good ole pork-n-beans in front of me
Eating till I was stuffed-
Happy and swinging my feet

A Black Woman's Need

Tell me what you see when you look at me? With my phat ass, luscious lips, and voluptuous hips, you think that mean you can disrespect me from your lips. No doubt am I everything that you want and need in a Black queen- but how you should treat me remains to be unseen. I am like no other, beauty and wisdom deeper than you'll ever know. Without me in the world, where would you go? I've been scarred in and out by you, and him, her and them. I have an attitude and you think I'm crude, a bitch, a broad that thinks she's the shit.

No my brotha- I am your mother! So when you come at me wrong it's a sad song because our mothers, mothers, mothers, mothers taught their sons right from wrong. So when you come to me and see a phat ass to fuck do you wish to know what I know about the world and such? Do you wish to know what I can do to help you get through, or is your intentions to be hurtful, mean, and just as crude as my attitude. I'd like to know why I must give myself to you. Yea some of us may want money, but shit, it's not as if were being treated decently by you. I'm disappointed and flaunted as I let you take me the way you want me but deep inside I know I'm the bigger fool because I let you have me.

Understand black man that this is our land. We slaved to make it so we need to grow and shape it. If we're fighting, disrespecting, and constantly mistreated by one another, Before too long I'm going to give my being to a race of another. Please know that I am a Queen- a Mother. And I want to love you as you need love to make you see. There is nobody that can take my place. No other women, no other race. I'm not being prejudice but I am being real. My being is to love, as my heart is to heal. You want me and need me to live, but in the way you perceive it you need to grow up and get real. I am to love- just as you are. I am to be respected and treated equally like our ancestors worked to make it this far.

Understand that I am playing the man, the woman, the father, the mother, the sister, the brother, and all the other. You come in when you want to, you go out when you want to, you take care of what you want to, you treat me the way you want to. Wondering why we are as independent and straying away. As time goes on and knowledge grows our hearts will be froze from the pain constantly exposed. I want to love you, I need you and so does the children and society. But positive recognition is in a different era that is not today's priority. Wake up and look around at what's become: women needing and desiring each other, to spare another scar. I wish to love and honor you as a King. But your means of royalty is a destined dream. Maybe next time around, a world I hope I see, we'll have our chance to be treated as a Queen. But right now the day appears only in a woman's dream.

This is a Black Woman's Need

Duckin' Down

I see the "thugs" on the street
Hurt to themselves
Starting all that beef, but stay in the street
Asking for the death sentence
Though- scared as shit

"Black told Ray-Ray you gon fuck him up!" Lil Man say
More problems today- More than yesterday
What we see you doing all day?
Duckin' down... you betta duck down bruh

Ray-Ray told Lil Man to let you know,
"If that nigga wanna pump we can do it any place. Fighting ain't my game, cuz if the nigga whip my ass I can't have niggas laughin' in my face. So Ima blast his ass, what he wanna do? Can't take it back my nigga, you said the wrong thing, now you're through."
You betta duck down homie and watch your ass.
There you go duckin'

All day long tryin' to make that cash
Don't know when Ray-Ray gonna pop up on your ass-
But you gotta increase your dough stash
You say to the lil dudes, "Watch my back, I'll give you twenty a piece every hour- holla when it's time for Ray to get gutta."
But when they roll out to go take a piss, Big Ray come on around and POP, POP, POP, the sound goes past your ears-
Damn he just missed

"Oh shit, that shit's just hearsay, why the nigga trippin'?"
What the fuck have you did?
Guess you better duck a lil lower man
This could be the day that your ass turns to sand.

Just your luck, Ray got knocked off
Missed your ass, you're just a lucky cause
But I hear sometimes you be runnin' your mouth
More gossip, more rumors being spread about
Just the other day, Lil Man got caught up spreadin' a shit of lies
So now he gotta start duckin' before he six feet under ground

Well... that's the way it is in these ghetto streets
Big mouths get big beefs
It's really funny though...
'Cause all yall "fools" forever duckin' down

What is Sistahood

What is Sistahood when we're set off by a stare?
When we look upon the black woman we are
It's not a look of admiration- but a glare of despair
What is Sistahood, when jealousy is a factor?
In which we look down on the beauty, we all share together

Not only do we act ignorant, but foolish to the fullest
Pissed because some of us doing well in life
When a clap of the hand should salute us
I get so tired of the eye-rolling, bitch-calling
Smart-ass remarks my sistahs say
Rather be a hater
When you can just congratulate

What is Sistahood?
When we've been segregating amongst ourselves
Sistahs, where is our love, where is our wealth
Black women PLEASE, hear me when I say
How disappointed I am that we're gone astray
My patience is ending- the bitchiness too free
How we act towards each other, is like an incurable disease

What's up with this idiocrasy?
Too much I see
Jezebels is how some of you are
As if you are the only star
I'm trying to understand the attitude
The behavior, the ignorance
The look in your eyes so crude

I just want unity between all of us, all of WE, you and I
Can you please help me find a way- for us to unify
We have children to raise, so we need to act right
Let them know we are love and set an example, despite-
The things we may go through- and the things we may lose
The things we may not have yet, but another person do
That inside us is a gift we can share, and show them how to use

We must love each other and band together

To help stop our races' corruption, and break free
It's not worth the BS and drama, and shame that we breed
But definitely a waste of time, when the world is so in need
So What is Sistahood? Really, I don't know
Eventually, I hope, the realness in it will show

Communities in Disaster- "Urban Defeat"

Every day on the news-
Someone has killed another in the hood
Every day on the corner-
A drug dealer, a pimp, an addict, a whore
Every day in our hood,
Blacks selling out their own people for money- to be ghetto fab-
And it's so damn cruel
Every day an application rejected, a child neglected,
A woman disrespected

We know we are judged by where we live, judged by education, judged by our skin. Doesn't matter what we have in our minds, or even how we feel inside. It's expected for us to stay down, but no more can we rise if we're constantly let down.

Girls age twelve, having sex all the time, boys age twelve, given drugs to sell. What's going on in their minds you wonder, the fear of the world outside keeps them under.
We get so caught up in "images" that we think the way some people "act", is the way it "is", the way we should live- who we are.

Don't get caught up- prove you are of fame; even when you feel you don't have a chance to promote your name. How many people from the ghetto have been able to make it known?
Those ones who worked hard- please give back; stay real, grounded, and strong.

We have nothing but want everything. Discrimination is against the law and part of our territory. We live on the streets, we sell our souls, we have no glory, we have no backbone. It's not free- we're not equal. If that was the case, why can't we get past our issues? Get knocked down every time we try. But the label placed on us says we're not civil.

Who would've thought Martin Luther King's dream would be reality? It seems to me nowadays we've gotten so far so they can shut out our complaints. But look where we are- where we always been. Yeah, it gotten a little better, but we still live the way we live- and it's all one big game:
They throw a little loot to single mothers in the ghetto; distribute a little drugs to keep them mellow- lazy, a criminal, dysfunctional.

Every time we stand up and claim our cause, they give a little back but we're still defeated- because: we won't demand what is ours- and stop being who they want us to be; create our own lives and take control of our destiny.

Yet we still live the way we live and it gets worst in our spirits and minds, and defeated we are.

Survival, to Struggle, to Unite, to Overcome

All my black people stand!
Take a stand for yours in this land-
Take a stand for those who have struggled to overcome our races' defeat.
Take a stand for all those who lives have been sacrificed to better yours.
From survival, to struggle, to unite, to overcome-

The black race has made strides that you being black can't imagine:
Survival of the abuse, torture, and death of slavery.
Struggled through "by any means necessary".
United for our freedom to vote, better paying jobs, education, homes and resources to live
Strides that has made us overcome!

Black people have took a stand and made it.
Made it for us, made it for all, made it "for real".
So when I see the streets of black leaders and activists littered with the lost and broken;
It saddens me-
'Cause I know they didn't fight and die for us to live like this and be.

They did these things so we can have the best of life.
The best of life we can only make for ourselves by-
Surviving the struggle to unite and overcome-
For a common goal...
The goal to be undeniably FREE

Love in Unison

To a world infested with hatred and cruelty
To those whom breathe in life as we breathe
To families in crisis that won't feel the touch of love again
To the lonely souls whom pray the loneliness will end
To those who stand up and give their life
And those who are innocent- caught outright...
In the eyes of Satan and his will for destruction

Perfection of evil lives in those who take life with obsession
What are we to do when we don't know what's to happen?
We live each day like its eternity
But one day you see that thousands can cease
Vicious are the men whom Satan possess
The Creator is in battle to defeat Satan's plan
We've sold our souls for what's unknown
Feeling that the prize is to each-its-own

We forget each day to live and love together
The unison of warm-hearted, consciousness makes life better
If you can, please understand what I say
The love from our heart, lights the way
We have to come together and not let our world fall
Freedom is the souls that makes it home

So let's win this battle and make things right
There's much wrong going on- where is the light
Please stop and think of someone else
No one lives in the world by themselves
Who are you? Do you know?
Find out and see
Let it change you forever so you can conceive-

That what they do to us, you do every day
To those who you profess to love and care
- But betray
So let's stop the hatred and begin to be
The unison of love that the world truly need

Frantic Reality

Frantic Reality

A Heartbreak, a Heartache, an Earthquake
For Heaven's Sake

Let ME Be Free
From the world and its hypocrisy
For me to see
Shallowness, hollowness, horror, pain
Ashamed of the ground, where I remain

To see a clear sunny sky on a May day
The trifle of humanity consumes every place
And drowns in disgrace
In what we call the human race

Illiteracy, why?
Education swamps on the rise
Programs, demands, equality cracks it up
The reprimands of our existence, everybody fronts

Chosen are few, although many are called
I pray I am of the chosen ones
And not prey fall
To the demise of it all

Exhausted by Humanity

What is the problem- why am I mad
When someone fuck with me
Blood rushes to my head
If it's really me, then why can't I see?
The damage that it's doing to me, personally

Then again, it just may not be
The real me is kind, gentle, and sweet
Not the part of me that I've tried hard to deplete
An exaggeration, but is truly what it means

Huffing and puffing
All day long
Trying to take heed of the blessings
And stay strong

What is the problem?
What does this mean?
Am I diminished to the ferocity?
Of life's hellish defeat

Do people really get it-?
Just don't fuck with me
Rub me the wrong way- fuck with my head
Go ahead, you'll find yourself in dread

I'm a lover- not a fighter
A winner- not a loser
To forget that all of this is surreal
I'm better than the choosers

What I believe
Is what I conceive
My talent unspoken
The player of dreams

For real, the problem
Is humanity
So if I'm angry and want to fuck shit up
The blame isn't on- Me!

Empty

Empty, I feel when I'm in the middle of it all- alone
Unfulfilled, incomplete, void
A wash out
Empty from what I was stripped, abused, used, and had
I've been stark-raving mad
Trying to fill the emptiness, flushing out the dread

Empty
Unfulfilled, incomplete, void
Violated, isolated, trying to shout my claim
Claim to be fulfilled, loved, and be reeled into the world
Not a sunken deep hole, snagging and ripping my soul

Emptiness
When you have nothing and no one around you
For you
Stare in the mirror and you will see
Someone staring back, giving you all you need
Which is you- just believe

Stress

No money for the rent
Phone disconnection
Being late for things that are necessary in living
Stress

Helping others who won't help themselves
Burden of the nonchalant character
Trying to stay patient and remain sane
Stress

Oh, I'm a fool
It's not the end of the world
Recovering from desperation of how life whirls
Stress

Taking time to relax
But worries and doubts tenses you to pain
Dying crying trying to maintain
Stress

Spirits of Love, where are you?
Come through me and take it all away
If not, I may not live to see another day
Thoughts of death, loneliness, helplessness,
Destroying one self
Why?

Just stress

Life and Pain

I feel like my life is over
Now as I speak
Just flew away and left me
To scream, and rant, and weep

Lately it has been nothing but pain
I feel so alone- I feel I shouldn't remain
Alive and well, or hurting like I do
And the drop of my tears...
Falling each day, in and out
I can't live like this
I want to take my life

I have to pray every day
Hopefully the Creator will hear me and bless me all the way
By answering my prayers
Taking away my fears
And help me to live, like I want to live

Suicide

Ocean breezes- crisp, cracking, smacking my nose
Freezing to the bone, but feeling good- a refresher indeed
Seagulls flying as high as mountain peaks
Singing songs in my heart as if it relates to what my mind is tormented by

Only here alone I am
Alone to fear myself
The rocks and water and gulls and sand
Here to keep me safe
My mind's icy like the chill of the wind
Darkest thoughts in my head about how and why I want life to end

So damn simple to just do it and get it over with
But the crashing of uplifting, hard, violent waves makes me think better of it
A slit of the wrist-
But then I'd be found
I want to be forgotten and hear no wondering sounds of the loved ones left behind
I can go to the shoreline- with razor in hand
Let the waves carry me off the damp mushy sand
Or slit my throat, my wrist- a gunshot to the head
To take myself out of this misery, I rather be dead

I hope no one hates me
Like I hate myself
Everyone knows my stress to battle
So they may think I've run from it

Well here I am drifting
Sinning and praying to go to heaven
This doesn't hurt so bad
Maybe sooner would've been better

Nobody Knows

The pit of my soul before it all
Couldn't stand to be alive
The prize of "life"- unreal

I can't say that I've loved myself
Lonely in the shadows of others
Drawn into desires
Wanted love that in which I hadn't had
Preyed upon by Satan's plan
Nobody knows

I only wanted to feel the love I never knew
I look at the cycle of my life and see
The love hadn't exist in me
I've been used, assaulted, fornicated upon as a child
A fucking alcoholic
Nobody knows

Not being understood
And that's what you want most of all
Nobody knows the misery
I wanted to love me and love the world outside of my life
But hardly noticed, with any voice to speak-
Then desperation set in-
Became my motive in the madness I was in
Nobody knows the pain I was in

When You're Fat

You feel abnormal
You feel unwanted
You feel unloved
When You're Fat

Your stomach has handfuls of rolls
Your legs rub together and get black in-between
You lose your breath just walking up the street
When You're Fat

People look and gawk
They talk behind your back
You're looked at as below par

You don't look in the mirror
You don't get on a scale
You don't bother going out to have fun
'Cause you can't fit Your fat ass in something to wear

You get left out
You get no play
You feel like Your fatness will make you disappear one day

So you eat some more
Till you hurt deep inside
You fail your health
Because emotions you're trying to hide

When You're Fat
It's hard
And it'll be worst the next day
So look at yourself in the mirror... And Love
Don't get comfortable being this way
Get your fat ass up and start being not fat today

Fuck You

How can we get real, if you don't tell me how you feel?
Knowing that you avoid my calls, don't tell me how you feel at all
Learning about your every desire- that's what you say I must do
How can I possibly do that- if you won't let me get close to you?

Lies, cheating, heartbreak- for heaven sake
I'm surprised I'm not dead for fucking with a dude like you
I get stalked and harassed
And an STD for going raw with you

How I get myself in this shit?
I might deserve it for shit I did
But I don't care. It ain't right
And I don't have to put up with it

Girls... watch out for a guy who has....
A wad of money, but no place to stay
A nice ass ride, but no means to pay
Living with mama or no stable place
Say they'll buy you shit, but first they wanna hit

That playa look- fools is what they are
Acting like a superstar
Fuck that shit, I wanna real man
Give me your work, home, and cell phone number
Respect me, know me, love me
Maybe later you can stick it in
But until then...
Fuck You!

The Worst Dude

The worst dude is different than any other man
Whether black man, white man, or Hispanic and
He's the worst of them all
The one that drops his drawers
Tell you to crawl
And come suck his balls

He's maybe good-looking
With a nice stick
Independent, looted up, with a bunch of sad chicks
Hardly takes you out
And calls you late at night
Knowing the coochie tingling
Cuz he hit it right

You try to hang with his friends
But you're just another lush
So there's always an excuse
That's the way he fronts

He always says-
Don't you trust me?
And you do, don't you?
Baby don't do this
Because he's going to hurt you

They play mind games
For your heart, love, panties, pockets
They roll out when you get too clingy
And they say shit ain't goin' right

Scared they are- what is there to lose?
For real, a lot- like Life
For messing with the crazy one
Thinking she's a fool
Messing with a sick one
Now you got that shit... OOooooo

The Worst Chick

The worst chick is slick
And mentally not right
Play like honey for your money
Instead of your heart
Give you good loving
Until she tears you apart

IF she ain't digging gold
Then she feeling a lil old
Wanna stay young forever
Acting like she bold
When really she in need
Of love and affection
But so much past baggage
She constantly projecting

Let's not forget Ms. Rachet
Blowing up the spot
Watching too much housewives
When a husband what she want
But too many baby daddies
She got too many seeds
Hoeing and towing dis-ease
Down and out, indeed

The worst chick should be alone
And do some work on self
Before she think about a man
She need to learn to love herself

Want Some Ass?

Part 1

Images of Death

In no way anyone want to live with any STD; it's the sin that flows in the blood that's used to keep you functioning. Do you ever think when you do what you do? Knowing the possibilities of what could be, but really do you?

It fills you up with poison from something that seems so free. But now images of death infects your mind and drowns out your psyche.

God knows the souls who are feeling the sick inside. But truth brings them to the reality of their chosen lifestyle.

Stop the sin and save your Soul-
'Cause if it's lost, everything goes.

Want Some Ass?

Want some Ass?

Part 2

Getting Down

Today young folks just floating away
Just looking to abuse that ass
Not knowing that getting in that ass
Can make life end real fast

Penetration, the floatation, rhythm nation
Of the body grinding, booty shining
Smackin' it, flippin' it, rubbin' it down
Don't know what's going on down in the royal crown-
Of the ass that you pound
The pipe that make you sing out loud

Wanting some ass can get you fucked up
Niggas, bitches, fools break the rules
Know what I mean?
The sex seems to gleam
Ooo, Ahh, want to do it again?
Next time let my friend join in- there you go again

Spread your shit- know who give it good
That one that does can leave you dirty and crude
You want some ass huh? You love to fuck?
You love the penetration? You love to suck?
Getting that ass is sometimes hard enough
Don't be stupid and get your ass stuck
With some eternal bad luck
Want some Ass?

Only the Lonely

I remember feeling so alone one day. No one to come to my rescue in the night when I felt I couldn't bear being alone anymore. Hearing my own cries while the tears fell slowly down my face, I thought that my pain would never end and my tears will never stop their flow.

Lonely is a feeling and a being that no one wishes to go through. People destroy themselves to avoid that feeling. The pain they feel when they're lonely shows in so many ways, that evil preys upon them in an instance.

Evil loves the lonely.
Evil loves the deadness inside those who feel like they're the only one on earth and everyone else is just an illusion.
Evil preys on their weaknesses and their desires.
Evil can take over a life and make things a bigger illusion when they think their desires is met.

Don't be fooled. It's kind of odd don't you think? To have no one at your side one day and all of the world in your being the next. When your desires have been met it's like all of what you've wanted and wished for has come true. Don't be fooled. That's just the evil lurking around the corner trying to cast its spell on you. Make you a part of the hate that will forever live in our world. Make you think you're becoming everything you want to be, but becoming nothing of who you really are.

It's overwhelming the thought of being the center and not the outsider. It's lovely too. Everyone is now in love with you. You have a man/woman, you have acceptance by peers, you have everyone in your face that in the beginning wasn't there. You think you're happy, you don't want to let it go, you drop the little guard that you had and let your vulnerability show.

Don't think I don't know. I do better than anyone who thinks they know me. 'Cause I was an outsider, a castaway, someone who wasn't worth anyone's time of day. You know it's still so hard to think about, when I remember my past. Kissing ass to be part of the clique who was always fast; never did I look to see what it was doing to me- evil leeching on to me, God tugging me to keep me whole, my emptiness inside never had been shown.

A product of the 90's- a hellish decade in deed; people dropping dead like flies from gunshots, drugs, and disease. Forever will the cries go on. There was no snow on Christmas just the cold of night; the wind blowing fiercely just trying to stay warm and keep tight. I have so much to say to the world's people whom gone astray.

Only the lonely feel like life is nothing than a song- a comparison to words that aren't even yours to own. You can't say that love will never come your way; you can't say that your heart will never be heard- from one who's crying for your heart in return.
Only the lonely wakes up and seem so depressed- like life will never be nothing more than stress. But indeed they lack the knowledge of how much they're blessed.
Only the lonely goes into the dark, goes around trying to find the image of their destiny, trying to find exactly where their souls should be.

Only the lonely can't get it together: no one to push them, no one to lean on, no one to comfort, no one to cry on, no one to laugh with, no one to make love, no one to say, "You're all I think of"; no one to hear the voice you yearn to hear, no one to say, "I missed you while you weren't here", no one to tell you that you can do all that's in your heart, no one to tell you that no matter what your still among the stars; no one to kiss, no one to hug, no one to walk with, no one to bug, no one to play with, no one to lay with, no one to bathe with, no one to stay with, no one to love you, no one to care; while I'm saying all of this that you feel may be you, you really don't have a clue... you're breathing aren't you.

You're here today, can't you see. Touch your nose, your chin, and your feet; walk a lil, dance a lil, smile a lil, jump a lil, shout your name, go around and claim your reign. If you were alone, you'd never be; to see these words and relate to the knowledge that I speak. As long as you are here you'll never be alone, no one is lonely, GOD is here to answer your call. Believe in yourself and HE will have faith in you, believe in you, and help you achieve the positive notion that lies within you.

You were never alone; you always had someone or something by your side. Please know that if you look above the sky and say a little prayer, the spirits of love will say back to you "You were never alone, we've always been here..."

As long as you have you, you'll never be alone. No one is lonely, just answer your call. Believe in yourself and have faith in you. It will help you achieve the transormation of love that lies within you.

Respect

R- Regard that it's not all about you; you've grown to understand this
E- Empathy to your character by showing dignity and not hostility
S- Suppression of the ego and emotional attacks, using diplomacy and tact
P- Promote an attitude that will be beneficial to you and the circumstance
E- Effort to stay cool, though inside you're ready to blow
C- Consideration of the actions that will cause an impact
T- Temperament and a strong mentality to face wrong

It's crucial to respect, for disrespect leads to cruelty

Needs

Needs:
Focus
Work
Money
Time
Health
Knowledge
Wealth
Believing and loving myself

*Focus on the Needs- the Future- the Dreams
*Work to take care of the Wants- the Needs
*Money molds the situation- to do what I want and need to do
*Time- to Implement- Start- Process and get through
*Health I need to Live- to Love- to Give
*Knowledge is my Backbone- for when the BIG PICTURE shows
*Wealth is my Drive- to make it all come alive
*Believing and Loving myself- is to know my worth in life

The Real World

As time goes by, I get out of denial about the fact that-
Life ain't easy; ain't a damn thing free
Growing up wanting to be grown
Not knowing the rude awakening life had to offer me
Not thinking about the effects that I now have to change
What I don't have now, I'm part of the blame

I'm hurt, humiliated, and disparaged of myself-
Rollin out, having fun, putting life on the shelf
What I do now, depends on how my future will shine
'Cause life's a bitch, then you die- true words to live by
Work hard and do right
Maybe later you'll live a better life

I have experience, so I shouldn't be dumb
I'm mature, though I kick my own ass on the floor
Gaining knowledge is hard, when you half listen to shit
Experience it, fuck up, and maybe then you'll get the hint

Back to life's a bitch and then you die-
You work to live, you live to die
This is what I know
In this world, doors open and caskets close

The choice is yours, while you're here
Learn to behold- learn what it is
The real world is yours, it's what you make it
Create your reality, and no one can take it

What the Hell Am I Gonna Do?

What the hell am I gonna do?
I need to do so much
Like lose weight, be a good mom-
Keep my job, and such

I'm tired of being tired
I'm tired of the strain
I'm tired of hearing myself all the time-
Complain, Complain, Complain

Feeling ashamed- down and out
I know on the real that ain't what life's about
So what the hell am I gonna do?

I don't wanna struggle with this shit no more
I don't wanna cry about this shit no more
I feel stronger, but like I wanna die
I want so bad to get through- so I try and try

In the meantime- while the stress is still grand
Though inside of me- I must say- that the tiresome is bland
I'll admit that I have a problem, issues, etcetera-etcetera
But what the hell am I gonna do to make this shit get better

Fuck! Hell!
I really don't know
But I'm determined
So that means, I'm not gon' let it roll

So what the hell am I gonna do?
Become the part of me that is the truth
Become the person I want to be
Manifesting the spirit of love inside of me

Dev-eyes (Devil's Eyes)

Dev-eyes:
Looking through the Devil's Eyes
Eyes of Self-Destruction
A trap on your mental and emotional state
A trap on your soul and spiritual stake
Destroying the things only love can bring
Attaching you to mysterious things

A spirit wandering
Lost in themselves
A spirit trying to find a place for themselves,
Unconditional love and all they need
So they can live where love can be

Having no conscious
Don't know the reasons why
Wanting to disappear although you deny
Subdued non-understanding reason
Of why you hurt inside

Inside the Devil's Eyes:
Pain, Heartache, Grief, Lost, Lust, Impatience, Greed, Hate
Blasphemy, Unfaithfulness, Lies, a Thief, Anger, Resentment
Ignorance, Selfishness, Adultery, Murder, Unloving, Uncaring
Inconsiderate, Shameful, Hurtful, Blaming, Disloyal, Evil, Loathsome,
Stressful, Frustration, Unacceptable, Negativity, Displaced Emotions,
Self-Destruction, Life-Destruction, Soul-Destruction, HELL!

DEV-EYES:
Looking through the DEVIL'S EYES
Eyes shown through the darkness, places unknown in the heart for-
Soul, Love, Life, Happiness, Prosperity, and Spiritual
DESTRUCTION

Don't get caught-up in disguise, because looking through the Devil's Eyes
can be your demise

Love Lust and Longing

Can You/I Know

Umm, baby, can you feel it?
Can you feel me inside you?
Can you feel me beside you?
Can you feel me?

Umm, baby, can you see it,
Can you see me in love?
Can you see me as yours?
Can you see me?

Umm, baby, can you hear it?
Can you hear me whispering your name?
Can you hear my moans?
Can you hear me?

Umm, baby, can you love?
Can you love me to the fullest?
Can you love me completely?
Can you love?

Umm, baby, I know
I know you want it all
I know you know the truth
I know

Clear View from the Distant Truth

Feeling your presence next to me
I feel love- I feel you
Am I supposed to ignore this
The fact that I'm far away- yet so close to you
So close, in heart
It's love at first sight

With you tonight, I'll share my world
My body altered, my head in a whirl
Fantasies, imagination, with just a look from you
Am I destined, tonight, to meet my king
Is tonight the night I live within my dreams

Will we grow together, merge in our love
Bloom seeds of our happiness into the world
Exactly what this is, is a mystery
It's factual that I haven't even met you yet
The grins and stares says in some way we'll connect

But this is how it be up in the club
Not usually will I meet someone in here, looking for love
Who knows, God knows, I'm yearning love-
A mate, a king- a helper of child bearing-
And royalties of living our dreams

But still, who knows
I just want it to flow
So come on over here
Let's get to know

Come to Me

Every time I see your face and visualize the image of us
I can't see how you could want her anymore
She's not all I can be-
So tell her to release you so you can come to me
By the time we make love, I'll have myself in your heart
Thoughts of me will play in you
You want me- ravish my body when it's time to lay me
I'll make you holla until you roar
You'll hold me tight and won't ever let me go
You'll tell me I'm all you ever wanted in a queen
So be with me- set free-
Come to me

Seduction

This brotha over here
Mackin' while I'm relaxin'
Butterfly kisses- eyes entranced
Full of romance, but then again
He trying to show his dick- what a tripp
What's up with this?
I don't know, but I do feel bullshit
But is it? Why? Man I don't know
Want to just get up and go
Not have a chance to let the seduction grow

In his eyes, I see...
Nothing
Games, plays, I'm a stray... of which he may want to lay
Have I not earned the privilege of this fusion?
Is the passion and intrigue just delusion?
Have I been seduced only for some time to kill?
My lips- they spilled...
Over his- I was filled...
Seduced, by his seduction

For So Long

So many times I thought of love we could share
So many times I wished that it were I there
So many times I dreamed of us making love
So many times I wondered what you thought about us

For so long- I've longed and yearned for you
The feeling of my heart beating for you
God I wish I could be with you-
Touching you, holding you, loving you, oooo

For so long I've craved for you
Seeking to find where I live in your mind
If only I could have you as mine, just one time
That's all you'll need to decide to be mine

Won't You

I know what you're trying to do to me...
That look you're giving me; why you trying to seduce me?
You know I'm horny, why you wanna do this to me?
Licking your lips like you're thinking about kissing my...
Drinking me up till you're full of my Love
Your eyes are penetrating me
For I need to be close to you
Have you become one with me
Won't you?

Desire seem to ooze from you
Telling me that I need to pull you much closer
Have an encounter that drives me deep into your aura
I feel as though I need you some more
Its confusion the illusion I have...
Of the moment I laid my eyes on you
I trust the fact that my heart went a pit, a pat
When you stepped over my threshold
Desire seeming to come from you, to bring me close to you
I want to need you
Won't you?

5 I Want You

Every night I dream of you
When daylight comes and I don't see you
You stay on my mind all day long
That I can't help but to call your phone

I want so bad to pick up the phone and say:
"Baby I want you, come over right away"
But it's so sad 'cause I know you belong to someone else

So what do I do- just wait for you
Stop simply being in love with you
Just throw out, my dreams coming true-
The reality of me, loving you

So what do I do to turn the key
To start you up, so you'll come to me
Not no more, in my sleep
But in my bed every night, making me weak

I know you want me
You know I'll rock your world
Don't be scared...
Just leave your girl

Intoxicating

You're intoxicating...
Even though you make me sick
I still drink you up, I can't get enough
Fill my cup, with that of you
That makes me light-headed and queasy
Feeling I need to back away
But damn you make me feel so good
Feeling like I need to take you in
Like I'm a drunken fool

You're intoxicating...
I hate what you do to me
I hate how you make me feel
I hate that the chemistry with you
Is what I want to fall into

My head is hurting
My stomach aches
I'm going to throw up
From the love we make
Your love intoxicates

Love, Lust and Longing

Could it be that I'm in love with me-
Which has brought me to the reality-
That I'm in love with you

My shape, my hair, my assets, my flair
I melt into your likings
Diminish all the past...
For I have what has been held back too long
Life has brought me back to the reality
Of how I've always wanted and needed you most

Lie down for a while
And let me pass you out
The way you make me scream
I wanna make you scream and shout
I know I got the skills
But your ass sprung out

Convulsing with your thrust
Loving each other and loving our lust
If only things would be this good
I'd keep you for a lifetime...
And every day we'd lay, praying we'll keep it this way

Here we are, laid side by side
You turn to me and begin to grind
Your fingers graze my breast
As your soft lips caress mine
Your hand snakes down my back
Making me arch my spine

You look at me- like destiny
Your future with me- you can see
For I am the woman that got your heart...
And turned you out
Now your heart and soul are a part of mine
And that's what loves about

Love Mystery

Just as much a mystery as me
Denying the fact that truth will set us free
You expose you, as I expose me
Take a stand on what is meant to be

I may be foolish
I may be a lonely woman on the roam
But if I come to mind 3x's
Baby I'm on a roll

Stay sweet as I feel you to be
Sexy as I see you are
An essence to reflect something I want
Let us reveal this passions' intensity

As we solve the love mystery

Casanova

Ok, you know how we play, when we want what we want but don't want to give shit in return, and in the end we get fucked and burned. You feel me? Don't think that it can't be you. You still have a heart too. Don't you?

The mess and distress that you give so freely- do you really feel like you deserve respect as well as dignity? Mentally you have no feeling, physically you do. You stupid ass fool don't you know that your brain is the chosen tool to use.

To give what you are going to get, may not happen so fast, but one day somebody is going to fuck you hard in the ass. You're so invincible, you can't be touched, but before too long you will ignite and burn from those whom heart you struck; pierced, split, made them a bitter one. Do you feel good about how you fucked a good one for the chosen one?

So smooth and sneaky, iced-out and shining, wining and dining, got the kitty purrin' and callin'; a few moments here and there, a few dollars that you spare. The words that you say to that special lady makes her look into your heart, in your mind is where she ought to be, so she can see that this Casanova like to play with the mind and get into the poonie.

To all of you, you know who you are. I have a feeling after you read this you will be fucked from afar by the one who you feel is your shining star. You won't know what hit you, but in the end, I know you'll say, "Damn Love told me this shit will happen one day."

Thoughts of a Side Chick

Sometimes, when I lay in my bed I feel dread because you're not here. Wishing I could feel your body next to mine; your soft caress, your fingertips, stroking my kitty as she purrs.

Damn it's not fair the way things have to be, wanting you as badly as I do isn't helping the rage of eroticism in me. Sure I feel like what we share can't be denied, but how I wish we could be open, damn I hate to hide.

Ok, here we are, still no opportunity. So what am I to do; suffer wishing you could take me to ecstasy? Damn your lips I crave all the time, for your tongue inside them as they touch mine them. Still I can't help but feel the need to have you down on me. Clinching my thighs around your head as your tongue penetrates me.

I close my eyes and envision you- that's all I can do until my need for us making love comes true. I guess just wait for the opportunity with you and enjoy the pleasurable experiences, the times I do spend with you.

Damn it's a shame, my love is with you, and my kitty is yours; so why do I have to wait to give both to you. That's life- gotta deal- but I wish I wish I wish that this can be whenever, wherever, whatever.
But I know one day it'll be for real.

The Affair

Whisper being the caress of your breath on my breast
Enticing me with the succulence of your bottom lip
The flow of the rhythmic movement of our lips
Singing melodies of love to be made in bliss
Try and move from my air and see what you'll get
Don't get me upset 'cause you're trying to neglect-
Don't let me beg because soon you'll be the dog on his knees
Don't let me have to get you straight for moving away
Don't think I can't find where your fantasies lye

As you know the climax will hit you
As you're spasmodic convulsing, orgasms array
As you now try to hold it in, I make you let it go
As of next week, this time, this place, different pace

I am assured that I can give you:
All desired as this saga continues
All pleasures you've fantasized
All of me that you want to have
All of me that you have to beg to stag
All over you, I will be
All over the affair
And I'll be forever dreamed

What You Gonna Do?

Just this to tell you a little something about you and me...

Now, I didn't notice you and wasn't too fond of you
But what was inside you that edged you to proceed
Is what I feel in me- through you- I need

Now listen...

When I announced my being in love with you
It scared the shit out of me, yet made my heart soar

Damn it you, how did you get a hold of me
My heart was stone- my love on hold
Not letting anyone, anymore get between me

And here you come through the door
Your macking move- your charming ways
Told me whatever I wanted- there wasn't a price you wouldn't pay

Now here I am, a lovesick puppy
Down on her knees wrapped around your ankles
And begging...
Please baby baby please

You got your girl
Now what you gonna do?
I've fell in love
Now what you gonna do?
Never thought it'll be
Now what you gonna do?
Let me love you as you'll love me
Or leave me- 'cause of my love for you?
Oh, now you playing games
Honey, karma a bitch... don't be a fool

Out of Sight, Out of Mind

I can hear it in your voice- the despair
Willing yourself to stay and hold on
When what you want is to let go

I know I can be a little tough on the brain
What is it you still need or want from me
That helps you to maintain some feelings for me
I know I can be a magnet with my sexuality...

My divine sense of living,
My aspiring soul,
My beauty flowing
My uniqueness growing

Your eyes seem to wander around me
Your minds in a boggle as you try to piece me
Sometimes you got it right-
Most times you hunch your shoulders
Trying to portray me as...

Out of Sight, Out of Mind

A Way Love Goes

You're sitting at home and feeling alone, looking at the phone, and listening at the door for your lover to come home?
That's a way love goes

When it's six am and the alarm went off again, you're asleep on their side of the bed, in your dreams you're thinking they're there...
You wake up and look over, shaked up because it's not over
They're over the others' house again
That's a way love goes

The other hits you up and laughs in your ear, in the background that familiar sound that's irritably humble to hear, and finally you realize that this is your known fear.
That's a way love goes

You're deciding what to do; you're pissed even more as you feel your emotions come through. Trying to hide your pain is what you're going to do; that conniving asshole f'd you. Is it over this time? Last time you said next time? Now here goes- you gotta let go.
Understand that's a way love goes

When they come in, and don't even bother to speak, you try to talk but your voice trembles, and it comes out weak. They look at you like you're crazy- like you did something wrong.
You go ahead and spit it out, and again they lie and give you a kiss; give you the good lovin' you missed the night before. As you lay there naked and stupid you hear a slam- they're back out the door-

... that's just a way love goes

Getting Over You

When we first met all I did was think of you
And after the weeks passed
I could've sworn I was in love with you

But the reality was that you never really wanted me
And it hurt bad to know that I was emotionally weak

Now what do I do when my tears flow
What do I do when I can't seem to let the memories go

How can I fight my thoughts of you
How can I get over the pain you put me through

I guess in time I'll figure it out
But right now I'm crying, trying, to get over you

Adultery

My love has all I'll ever need. Why would I want to hurt him? I know that you are as sexy as me, but do you respect the fact that he's going to love me for me- as you love what you see and what you wish to have sexually? Through thick and thin, for better or worst his heart I'm in. All you see is the woman you wish for me to believe lies in your dreams.

My love means the world to me. Providing me with all the things I've ever dreamed: Real love, and real support, and real family beneath my wings. To be with you would be just a fling, and that isn't my thing.

My heart belongs to the man who took me out of my pain; took me in and sheltered me from the stormy rain. To be with him is all I'll ever need. Respect me. Being with you is neglecting what I say. You may want to treat me like a queen, but what's in between is the love I give only to my king.

I see your print and it looks good to me. Your lips I could imagine kissing, but back when I was a different me. I like how your eyes penetrate my body, I feel you now inside of me. But I'm a happy woman, in love for sure. But let me get your number just in case I have to close the door. So I'll call you if it does, but please don't you change.

Damn you, adultery. Why you have to be a bad thing?

Fighting with Love

Like your friends you seem to be
When things get tough
You up and leave
Don't you understand the responsibility of love?
I gave it to you completely and out the door you go

That out there is what you want most of all
When I cried and called you didn't hear me at all
Eventually I knew I'd have to let go-
And when I did you felt the blow
But I was too tired- so over it- so drained
To keep up with your and my side of our love
Now it's over, and out the door I go

My sense of security had me fooled,
But all awhile I was securing you
Available for all your needs:
I cooked, and cleaned, gave support and what's mine in-between
How did I get so wrapped up in this fantasy?
I wanted to spend my life with you
I thought you loved me and wanted that too

Maybe you do, but not in the way I want love
'Cause the love I want and need only the Creator can bring
My mind has changed and living for me and mine means everything
With you I couldn't excel- I couldn't stay focused
I thought I was maintaining the love that was for me
But I now know better that love is a two-way street

I never gave as much of myself as I gave to you
Trying hard to be with you
Trying hard to make you my king
But that dream is still a dream

We fought and loved-
Cared and cried-
And must live with the truth-
That's it's time to say...
Good Bye

Only in Dreams

Dreaming as my eyes are closed and I'm lying peacefully in the night. I do not wake up for the comfort of his hold keeps me underneath sight. To wake up from the moment when he finally kisses my lips with real love; comb my naps and talk to me saying words that only in my dreams I hear of.

I do not wish to wake up, for right now he tell me he's in love. I can't contain the heartfelt notification that the Creator has sent from above. Only in my dreams lives the reality of the man I wish to adore me. So I beg to sleep a little longer and be happy that love is coming for me.

I start to turn as it's almost six am and my heart beats faster as the love in need begins to end. If only my dreams can really exist, then happy I'll be and forever in bliss. But life isn't that way- I used to try and make it for real. But we know better to keep dreaming when a rude awakening will soon be to deal.

My lover I love a million times, our kisses as sweet as Hershey kisses and children's smiles. But will that dream of mine be real before me. Will he adore me like I should be, and cherish me like I should be, and care for me like should be.

If only we can live within those pleasant dreams of love. Our hearts are in our head but as we express it, it all begins to shred- for the perfection of love is among the fantasy and living for it is our reality.

Ladies and Gents- On the Real- What's Up?

Say I was to be your girl, and you were to be my guy
Would you still call me after we first make love
Or would you make me cry?
Say I was to be your "one"
And you were to be my KING
Would you run away from me?
Just to avoid a RING

Is it just a fantasy?
That my heart yearns to have
Or is it that you're just too stupid
To truly understand
Can't you see that misery
Is to not have love
So why you keep on pulling away
Away from what is love

I wish I could see inside your heart and your mind
Maybe then I can understand, why it is you want to shy
Shy away from something good
Or is freaking what you do best
But have you ever tried to be
A one woman man, at best

I know that women be trippin'
And not trusting what you do
But man, why you be buggin' out
Because you afraid to lose?
Chalk it up as experience
Experience is the key
Not to ward off love and affection
But to learn what you don't want or need

Now let's get to superficiality
Or let's just keep it simple
Yall tripp me out thinking a model
Will make you more of a person
Appearances can be shady
Shady people are fake-
Don't go playing yourself, baby boy
Their hair, nails, and eyes, are just as fake

My ladies, my ladies
Oh, what am I to do with you
Women stealing other women's men
What do you have to prove?
Baby girl, it's a big ole world
Why you gotta front
Just 'Cause the dude look good and got a lil clout
He ain't always what you really want

'Cause you know deep inside you're wide open
Not just for him to lay-
Your heart and mind and dreams galore
Are open for love to sustain
But you keep on fooling and hating
Playing and faking, escaping
The realities of what life breeds
The love we all need

There is a message I'm trying to spread
Hoe ass women, and dog ass men
Freakin' around, and fucking up
Having STD's, spreading lies and deceit
For games and pleasures
Shame and pain
When will you see, that even though sin is in
LOVE IS HERE TO STAY!

Let It Go- The Past

I'm trying to move on
To another life, another love
But I keep stumbling over things
That I haven't put my finger on

Moving on- Letting Go
So hard to do
I'm trying to Let It Go- The Past
So I can see my future through

A married man, a fling
A longtime lover- A Baby Daddy, too
But my true desire is for the one
Who I can wake up to, with every sun

I see the possibility
I'm hesitant, but ready to jump right in
I'm looking through his eyes
Trying to see what's in his mind

Being patient isn't my strong suit
But I'll do what I gotta do
Let It Go- The Past
And move to what I know is true

You see the games I've played with love
Talking about the hurt of it all
But listening and looking at myself, I know
I gotta pack it up, bury it, and Let-The-Past-Go

It's hard to do when you're trying to get through
You see what's yours but the past is grasping you
It all depends on the patience and will you have inside
To take hold of what you know is yours- takes time

Be strong, hold on, and keep control
Burn it, bury it, pack it, ship it, kill it,
Take the Past... And Let it Go!!!!!!!
But first you must be willing to do so

Letters to My Love

Love Is

Love is something special
When two people put their hearts together
Caring for each other is not enough-
There has to be honesty, faithfulness, respect
And trust

Walking through the park, gazing at the stars and moon
Passionate kisses that make flowers bloom
Holding hands- caressing backs
Making love wherever as romantic as can be
Under the moon and stars, under the whispering trees

How you feel, the one you love should know
In so many ways, you gotta show
The love in the air, escapes from your heart
Sends recognition, right from the start

Making your love grow, more every day
The emotions of love, no one can take away
The love between two hearts, and souls bonded together
Real Love is true and must always be treasured

The Catch

Perhaps I was the answer to your long-awaited questions
Filling your mind with understanding
Feeding your spirit with love you won't expect

Say I was the piece of the puzzle
The one you searched in others to find
But scattered among a likely spread
I stood out like the sun among clouds

Perhaps it was love at first sight
Know that nagging feeling is telling you
"She's it"
"This is right"

Our Love – The Creation

Have you ever been in love
And it made you virtually sick
The feeling of that feeling
Is hard to forget
When it feel that way
You're grown up and understand
That when it's fo sho
Love is in demand

I remember my first love
I mean the real one
You feel me
Life was like a disaster
But heaven when he was near me
Being in his arms
Smelling him- feeling his touch
I didn't care one way or another
I loved that brotha so damn much

Until this day I feel the same
We're not together right now, but I'm not ashamed
In my hour of need I call his name
Our attraction and affection
Like a burning flame

I love that man and will always want him the same
Will only love him unless another comes my way
I'm not a fool; I'm just in love
He is too, but the mystery streams from above

My soul told me for sure that he was my one
He shines with a light
As bright as the sun
One day we'll walk together
Hand in hand

Together forever our love will stand

In Love with a Stranger

I'm in love with a stranger
He just came out the blue
When I saw him the first time, the thought lingered on
And I knew I would love him through and through

It's like trying to find the pieces
The puzzle so hard to sort out-
But you know that it'll be completed
In time, the picture will come about

I'm in Love with a Stranger
And I don't know what to do
I wonder if he knows- is my affection exposed
He's the Mr. Me of my destiny... my soul told me so
But since it's not clear I won't go too far
He sends my heart racing-
My mind bent on conceiving
The truth of what we are

I sometimes feel he knows too...
Just like I do
But it's a haze of doubt, confusion, and unknowing
What will truly come out

I'm in Love with a Stranger
And it appears to grow stronger every day
No matter what it seems or is to me
The feeling never goes away
I'm hoping one day we'll click
I'm hoping one day we won't miss the content
Of what it has been a green flag
Telling us to steam ahead

How did this come to be
The connection between us, surely is a mystery
I assume I'll find out one day and together we'll lay
With our future on the way- together

I'm in Love with a Stranger
And I feel he possibly is too
But how, when, why, and so-
I pray on my heart it's true

Fantasy

As a woman, there was one thing that I needed-
And that was the feel and the love of a good man
One who would love and respect me for all I am and who I am
And what I give him as a person- as the man I love

One thing that would make our commitment sweet- is the love we create
The way we create love will make the earth shake
Green with envy people will be-
Wishing they could have a love like we

It'll be him I care about and him I adore
As we grow in each other hearts and souls
We can't be broken by a jealous man or a woman's scorn
'Cause our love forever will always be bond

I'm waiting for you, who is what I want and need
I know this is a fantasy- not yet truth-
You'll take care of me like I will for you
No longer just a fantasy- but a dream come true

My Heart is Open

My heart is open to bring you in
To give you love that I know you need

Suggest that I be the one
Come find out that it's well to do
You need me and I need you

Start with holding my hand
Feel a bond that must be taken from there

Grow with me- old and gray
We want each other- we love each other
Let's have each and be whole

My heart is open to you
Take my love with all good intention
My heart is open... Come on in!

Just You

Man it blows my mind with the constancy of our emotions
How we hardly make up an equation of normality
In the depth of my heart, just knowing the love I feel, as though
I still speculate from not understanding
Why I can't believe the presence of you in my life
I greed for those lips of yours I thrive to caress
And no one but you I want beyond the mess

Baby, see, I'm your queen
Your lady
The lover of your dreams
Let's live out the reality
Complete the batter of our soul's quest
To find that love of infinity

I know you feel me
For we have the same feeling
Let me know what to do
Just say it, and - poof
When we part I know it's a need
When we come together I'm just so happy

Come on now and be strong for us
Help guide me to the places that's meant for us
So I can feel you out with no influence but God
Just you and me learning each other and happy
So sweet, collaborated to become whole
In such a non-typical, different way
Infinitely with-
Just you

The Love Was There

I'm thinking about you
I hope you're thinking about me
I called you on the phone
But of course you wasn't home
You must be coming my way

Then I hear you knock at my door
I open it and there you are looking fine as can be
With champagne and chocolate strawberries for you and me
We danced all night and I felt something strong
But I didn't know what it was...
You laid me down and made sweet love to me
Then looked in my eyes and said you loved me

At that point I knew... the love was there

Don't You Ever Wonder? Why?

Don't you ever wonder why I can't help but see you?
Calling you all the time, just can't wait to talk to you
Looking in your eyes at the end of my long hard day
Just feels me with life I can't help but say
I wonder why I love him like I do

I love you so much that my own breath starts to sing
When I'm in your air, it's like I'm flying with wings
Can't understand how one person could ever make me feel this way
But just telling me how many times I've been on his mind
Giving recognition of what my presence with him brings

Holding me with sweet assure
That I am his lady and he is my man
What we have will never end
Don't you ever wonder why I just love you?

No other man has singled me out for me
Common interest and goals and a life to grow together-
Happily
I never understood how it was that true real love began
I asked if you ever wondered why I love you like I do
But all I can say is...
Because you love me too

Love at Ease

Kiss me gently
Subtle
Serene
My eyes flutter as romance fondles me ever-so lovely
Needed I be in your arms, for you, I'll stay there

Seek unto my heart, giving you the love of me
Beauty of my spirit, gentleness, at ease
The moment you laid eyes upon this likeness of a queen
You knew I'd be the realest love you dreamed

Don't stay away too long
For I am spirit others long
However if you know what's right
You'll keep me in sight
And real love will stay in your life

Undeniable, forever, you and me
Love
Happiness
Connecting the souls
What a beautiful thing
Love at ease

Happy in Love

You make me so happy
You make me so glad
You bring joy in my life
You made me love again

And even if the road gets rough
I will be right here
And even when we argue
I'll never disappear

Although people may lie and hate
I will never walk away
'Cause honey I know our love
Will make it any way

For our love is deep as the ocean
Our hearts beat as strong as a drum
For you are my king
You are my "one"

To the Love of My Life

I knew you were my one from the day I met you
I'm just mad it took so long for me to get you
Now that we're together- not a day goes by that I'm sad
When you approached me
That sealed the fate that it would be us at last

You're the love of my life
The man of my dreams
When the world makes me scream
I think of your face, I think of your touch
My heart starts to race
Because I'm in love

We have so much in common, in common so much
I never had to be a rep- I can always be myself
I never had to change my affection-
You wanted it laid on thick
I never had to change my image -you loved me healthy and thick

You took my child- I took yours
You told me for yall I'd be the only one
You told me you loved me from the very start
I often wondered afterwards was I in your heart

You're the love of my life
I made a wish on you
I prayed every night that you'll come through
I prayed every night that we'd click in a way
That my heart will be restored, with your love in place

Well baby boo, this is for you
I wrote this a long time ago but I'm giving it to you
When I did, I didn't know
I just hoped it was true
That the love of my life would finally come through
And it would be you

Love Brings the Anew

Complimented by what you see
You see the real me, do you feel me?
Compress my heart to fill you in
Let alone my head- you to be in

Starting with your masculinity
The muscles, the strength, the idealistic identity
Next come the words you say to me
Still typical a man that can't express the intensity
Of what he feels
But not so typical as to show he's for real

Then comes the lover you definitely can be
The lover that rocks my world and keeps my knees weak
The lover that dawned on me at dusk
Made me scream your name in passion with every thrust

Finally comes your heart- you set free
Something that's hard to let go- you gave it to me
Never did I think your love could be so real
You feel so great in me, the love you instilled

How in the world did you ever come to me
How did I get you? I wish I could see
The plan for genuine unconditional lovers to click
In a world as big as this, one flitch, and we clinched

The Creator is the reason, and the spirits of love
They saw that we both was ready for love
And brought us together, set afar
So a new beginning could start with you and me
The growth of our love will prosper and we will see

The miraculous truth of the love we've dreamed

Our Love- The Reality

Our love is a splendid thing:
Something only the Creator can bring
Putting our hearts together to bond as one-
Live as one, love as one, and grow as one
When we look in each other eyes
We see a beautiful future that can't be denied
Romantic and exciting times we'll share
Together

Connected by soul who woulda knew it could happen to us
Finding a love in each other- providing for us
Soul mates are what we are
We fell in love from the start
It's been like heaven since that very day
Embracing in each other mind, body, hearts, and souls
And the goodness of our ways

Thank you Alighty for putting us together
Forming something that some people will never measure
A union of love because there could never be
A greater love for us as we've came to be

Fundamentals of a King

He has the desire in his eyes to succeed
Always on top of things, never caught slipping
Powerful strength that'll knock another out
Business first and later with the bouts

Deep dark eyes and lashes that speak to me
One look into them, I feel the power within him
His hands are warm- His mind is strong
He respects all that is important
He a leader, a protector, a supporter and all
Don't sweat the little shit just get back up when he fall

He got mad skills from experience in his young days
Break off knowledge so you could know the deal today
Wise and mature, he knows what he wants
He's all about Respect, Dignity, and Standing Strong

Character of a Queen

She defies reality-
With nothing but love
As she holds her family close
She get things done

She has the desire to conquer life
For she's the mother of us all
A queen in a woman showing:
Grace, Mercy and Love

She doesn't take too keenly
The ills of the world around
But is guided by her goodness
And in the light, she'll be found

She's the beauty that is life
Her strength is love
Her wisdom is knowing
Her heart is caring

For a good woman knows her worth
And knows to respect herself
Because life flows through her
And that is her true wealth

Seeds of Life- the Children

Celebrating Life

Today I'm celebrating my existence
When, how, and from whom I was conceived
Today I celebrate being alive
I celebrate the good times and bad

The victories and defeats
The successes and failures
The mistakes and lessons learned
Life

Here because my work is not done
Here because I have a purpose in life

I celebrate life because life is a blessing
Life is good
Life is me here- Living Today

Birth to Life (For Mom)

I've realized in my life
That I couldn't have made it in this life without you
Even though you let me go free
You've been there to catch me when I've fall-
When I cried and called

Throughout it all, from the oldest to me
I've realized that you were created
To produce "we"
Your birth day means as much to me, as do mine
Because if you wasn't born, I wouldn't be alive

You see, time goes on and children let go
Get their own lives and try to achieve their own goals
Even when we get displaced and miss out on love
We remember your birth day
'Cause without it, we wouldn't have been born

Mom,
I love you
Love you more as the days pass
Your sacrifices, patience, and grace
I would never take for granted

Your presence in this world
Rose me from a seed, into life
Your birth day means as much to me
As every breath I take in- my life

Back in Time

How many times have your mind floated back in time
To a place where childhood memories played in full...
Outside playing Double-Dutch, going to the ice cream truck
Plaiting your friend hair as she plaits her doll baby hair
Sucking on freezy pops, chewing on gum drops
In the afternoon sunlight

Ms. Mary Mack- slapping your hands together,
Messing up bringing laughter between the two
Kickball, Baseball, Tag and all
Was the way childhood memories played in full

How many times have your mind floated back in time
To a place where you were in the kitchen...
With your mom, homemade cookies, eating the dough
Flour everywhere on your nose and toes
Whipping the eggs, to make them rise
To smell the freshness and the taste of goodness
Open your eyes wide in surprise
How those childhood memories play in full

How many time have you closed your eyes
And let your mind float back in time
When you felt free and whole, innocent and bold
With life to behold
Wishing you were a child again when life was grand
And the real world was unknown

Don't you wish you could go back in time?

Remembering Childhood

Back in the day on a Sunday a sunny day, was a chill day. Lying on the pavement trying to shape the clouds; Soft winds blowing, tickling us with a smile. Going to the Corner Store to get the cheapest candy, walking miles and miles and miles, feeling real dandy. When you're a child it's so easy to live, all you give is the joy and energy within.

Buttercups, lollipops, catching bees in a cup, mud pies, playing with worms, oh did I love to feel them squirm; climbing trees free as a bird. Oh man I wish those days would come again... I wish I wish I wish I wish those good ole days had never end.

Lying back reminiscing of trees, swinging on my playground singing with the blowing leaves. Tag, truth or dare, hide-and-go-seek, volleyball, kick ball, racing down the street.

Slumber parties with my friends, talking about the things we share, boys in school and teachers we hate, talking about everything- staying up late. First dates, and school dances, first kiss, first romances, on the phone with your girlfriends talking about how the kiss was all you ever dreamed.

To grow up and reminisce about childhood bliss and the things I was blessed. My childhood was like a dream, not fantasy- but real, as it seemed. To be a child is a wonderful thing. Don't grow up too soon or you'll miss a true blessing.

The Worth of a New Birth

The worth of a new birth
Is hard to comprehend
The reproduction of who you are
The person that makes you live again

Whether it's your first or your fifth
You can never feel the same as before
The worth of a new birth
Give you a chance to live for more

People take the value of life too lightly
We feel like tomorrow will always be
But the worth of a new birth lets you see
Love is your new budded seed

Know that nurturing them to be their best, is the way
It will give them a reason to live the best way
For the worth of a new birth, is a gift to yourself
To make you live, and live- again

My Baby Gurl- Alexsus

Beautiful she is, a sunny day, a flower in bloom. She changes and grows and always evolving, but is still a little girl. As I watch her day in and day out my heart cries for that long day my mothering life began. It's not so simple in the way we take care of our own. I wouldn't have known how fast she'd grow, if it weren't for my mind to consume. She's wonderful in as many ways that can and cannot be explained. She's my breath, my heart, my life, my treasure, my being, and my gift from living.

Golden brown, smile that makes a heart melt in a sense that there is ever-flowing love in the air from this precious jewel. Attitude is ever changing for her mind can't remain in time as the world goes round. The strength in her ability to do and know and show and hold her own is aspiration that she can and will make it on her own.

My child, my best friend, the one who showed me her life is worth me living a million years and a million times to raise her over again. Each time different, more better- more strong. She's my spirit, my strength. A wealth that no amount of money can ever be compared, for a mother and child is everything there is to make up life.

I love, honor, adore, take pride in, care of, nurture, forgive, listen, learn, shield, be concerned, put my all into, and give my protection, affection, and motherly devotion to: the most profound gift of life. Raising a child is most women destiny. But I know that one day this moment will end but to live it right now is a blessing and so much more. For love between us is unconditional and pure. I'll give everything in a heartbeat to keep this moment alive. But life goes on and I have to cherish this time because one day she'll be a woman and with her own life, saying "See ya later- BYE!"

Her Mother- Her Model

I am her mother and her model
Although I wonder if I am any good
Do I make a difference in my child life?
But I see her grown up, with success and grace

I am her mother and her model
I want to teach her all the good I know
And help her through as she grows
Beautiful and strong I know she'll be

I pretend she's the princess and I'm the queen
We live in royalty, though it's still a dream
I feel like tough love will keep her on the right path
But really I don't know how long it'll last

I understand that I have to do, what I have to do
To make sure she grows up right, and get through
I tell her everything will be alright
I'll always be there and be in her life

I dream about us having a friendship like no other
And things will be great and we'll be there for one another
I hope I can be a good example of light in her life
Because that's my role for her in this life
As her mother and her model

Gift of Self

When he cries in abandonment as you turn your back on him. What kind of love could you possibly feel? Can you sacrifice yourself from the world that has meant more to you than your true wealth?

Don't deny them; come when they call. Always wanted to be wanted, now you're wanted and needed and it's too much to stand- but don't lose it all. That relationship is all you've ever needed, the one that's to live for- the world is to die. Don't let the precious time slip by.

Give unto them, what you get is more than you've ever imagined or known. He or she is your destiny, the heirs of your throne. If it weren't for them where would you be? Say you didn't have anything. You had to live on the roam; no job, no home, no money, no backbone. But the state cuts you a check, gives you something to live off because the child is to live for; but to the fools it's just free dough you believe someone owes.

Those who think that way will pay; as time goes by with the money that you think is owed to you, you'll neglect the ones that are true to you. And they may eventually cease and there will be nothing left to grasp, and you're left alone, in despair and aghast.

You wake up and everything is gone and all you have is the scorn from the night before when he needed you and you told "Shut Up!" and struck him to the floor. Now you look around and no longer can be found. Now what do you have to live for? Everything your ever really had is now gone. Then reality hits and you beg God to save your soul. And it feels like you're going through hell, but you're coming to terms of what you've failed.

Now here you are, have you let the wicked world go, gained the consciousness of what's yours to own? Stupid ones who haven't won't, don't, I doubt so. You try to redeem yourself, prove that you are worthy of reclaiming your lost wealth. So...

You go to church and pray and pray- nothing happens. You go crazy, you get depressed and stressed until you can't cope with the mess. You can't sleep or eat, you only seem to sex, smoke, and drink. You have nothing now. It's hell for real; you understand the truth, so what's the deal. You want to die, so you try.

As you feel yourself slipping into the painless unknown, you hear a voice say Mommy or Daddy and you can't speak- you've lost your tone. All you can do is take all the memories in, and it hurts worst of all knowing what you did. You began to cry when you look at her or him and beg the Creator to forgive you of your sins and plea for one more chance to start over again... for the greatest gift of self- Your Children.

Lil Brotha, Lil Brotha

Lil brotha, lil brotha
Tell me what is your way
Is your way to thug and play
To lay around and waste your life away

Don't you ever dream of a destination?
Don't your mind ever plan?
Or is being sedated- stuck- delusional
Is where you plan to stand?

Lil brotha, lil brotha
I'm afraid for you
Your life relies on self-respect and dignity
To keep you following through

If you steadily being a:
"Baby daddy, hustla, gangsta, drop-out, slacker or thug"
How will you ever have abundance and wealth?
And live the life you want

My mission is to help you see
That you can find your way
You aren't your past, or your pain
There is strength in you, to guide your way

Females are jewels, like the bling on your ring
Respect them and treat them like a queen
They just want to be noticed for their strength and love
And a lot of them, are just as lost

Educate yourselves about life
Ignorance is not a way
But a ticket to the morgue or jail
For an extended stay

Stay focused on being the best you can be
And work at it every day
You can and will be someone you admire
And not so easily pass away

Lil Sistah, Lil Sistah

Lil Sistahs who are lost
Tell me what is your way
The way you conduct yourself, shows...
Your spirit has gone away

When you do what you do
And open wide-
You feel degraded and disrespected
Honey, where is your pride?

Remove the mask
You're sure to see a star
But do you think being "nasty" and "ratchet"
Is who you truly are

A jump off, a side chick, a baby mama full of drama
A siren, a stripper, a porn star or thot
Is this the way a queen wears her crown?
Or where grace, sophistication, and decorum can be found

I know life is hard and men can be weak
But what do you think you'll gain-
When living in shame
You will lose your "self", with these dangerous games

I'm talking to you 'cause I been there- I know
Desperate for love, money and a place in the world
You're living carefree, but coping defeat
Being in a world chancing drugs, death and disease

Now be real with yourself
And tell me you are of more wealth
Such as real love, family, a home
Something to gain, that's truly yours

'Cause when you do, you'll seek the true you
And know love will light the way-
To the place in your heart- is where it all starts
And full circle, your life will shape

So turn around and walk away
Get out this game, before it's too late
And be an example, for love's sake
To another lil sistah whose life is at stake

Transcending
Thoughts, Letters and Prayers

(Written age 20-30)

Dear Divine Creator-

Below are my letters and prayers to the true creator of love, light and life. Whatever the name: the Creator, God, Almighty, Source... Written at different ages and stages... the Divine Creator of ME was always there.

A Prayer for All

Divine Creator I pray for True Love, Blessings, and Freedom of the Mind Heart, and Soul. I pray for Miracles, I pray for Respect, I pray for Strength, I pray for Health, I pray to Stop Evil, I pray we all Forgive, I pray that we Fight for the Right to Live. I pray for our Families, our Friends, and Us All... Divine Creator I pray for Your Light, Life, and Love... I pray for Real Freedom to come...

I love You!
I love my Children
I love my Mom, Dad, Sisters and Brothers
I love my Nieces, Nephews, Cousins, Aunts, Uncles, Grandparents and In-Laws
I love my Friends, Lovers, and Enemies
I love yesterday, today, and tomorrow
I love before life, during life, and after life
I love the past, present, and future
I love, love
I love me...

My health I really want to improve for millions of reasons and I'm going to really try and press harder to become healthy. As long as you keep me waking up every day; moving, seeing, feeling, smelling, tasting, hearing, and learning- I'm complete- and know I have to do my part to be here and live as totally as I can.

My baby gurl, I want to be closer to: I want to do her birthdays and go to the WNBA games and watch her children grow. Be there for her through life's pressures. I want her to love me as much as I love her and not be angry with me for what I couldn't be or do, because I know she knows we can have so much better and do so much more.
But all I can do is keep a roof over her head, clothes on her, and feed her, and pray that counts for something.

I have to say what I love in my life is:
You, Alexsus, Mom, Dad, My Siblings, My Family.
I love my ability to function, I love having fun and being young, I love my times with my lover, my silly phone conversations with my friends.
I love the fact that I have a big heart and a good head on my shoulders.
I love that I'm cool, funny, honest, and considerate.
I love that my mom and me are closer than I'd ever imagined
I love when I'm alone to gather what I love and put it on paper and not be distracted.
I love, I love that I'm a writer, and one day I'll be able to share my gift with the world.
I love that I'm living, although it's not where or how I would like right now.
I love that I have you!

Thank you for providing me with a mom like mine.
I love her sooo much, for so many reasons.
She more everyday show me how unique and special she is and I feel sometimes like I'm the luckiest daughter in the world. She's a woman with sense and dignity, and wisdom that goes deeper than most. She doesn't tell me what I want to hear but what I need and should hear.
That's love.

The worries of my future being bleak, strained, and non-existent is ever-present. Is it ever going to change and allow me peace-of-mind? I know I'm blessed more than I could imagine, though life still seems like such a

nightmare at times: not knowing if the beauty and wholeness of my life will ever be.
I know somebody out there feels the same way I do.

What am I going to do about myself?
Sometimes I think I've made something out of nothing- but it turns out all the same.
Today I look like a complete mess. Why is this?
I have on these terrible gray trousers, that once fit nice on me, this spandex shirt that keep riding and showing my gut, my thighs look like they're going to explode, my shoes shoulda been thrown away by now. My hair is an utter disaster, and I just look and feel like every method of getting me to a good weight of 165lbs and a size 12 needs to be taken.
I look around at these females who need to go change, and I look at myself in the mirror and saw I needed to too. I mean from the top of my head to the bottom of my feet.

I need to lose about 85lbs, get a new do, nails and feet done. Man... it seems like the list goes on and on.

I want to lock myself in a closet and die.
It's just everything in my life coming at me causing me worry, pain, conflict, irritation, chaos, everything that is hurting me mentally, psychologically, emotionally.
I have nothing but breath, air to breathe, and being able to breathe- all else is out of control. Unstable, perilous and on edge- and my whole being is right with it.
I try to hold in my emotions, hold back the tears, but the pain behind them hurts and stings my eyes as my tears fall.
I try not to eat, I try not to wake up at night and devour myself with food- trying to shut out the bad dreams. I try to be as nonchalant and non-thinking as before, but it's a part of me now. I try to remember myself and think of how I want to be, but it won't let me.
My love of myself I try hard to obtain is controlled by what's happening.
I never knew I was so "this". I'm trying to accept the blessing of life that I have- but by everything being so strenuous and mind-boggling and frustrating and unpredictable. I need something that'll help put all the pieces back together.
Is it you?

I'm tired of have the same feelings that I've had for so long.
It's ridiculous.
Am I feeling sorry for myself, or am I making a testament in doing something about this?
Frankly, it all feels like I'm feeling sorry, although I have an agenda to change. I don't want to feel like this, look like this, or act like this. It seems like everything about me shoot my confidence and self-esteem down: like I don't like myself until I'm quirky and funny; otherwise it's like this person who feels like she doesn't belong.
Who cares about fitting in?
I just want to feel comfortable around different people and places. I want to like myself and feel comfortable about what I do, say, act, and think.
Comfortable about the way I look, seem, and feel.
I want to be who I am inside.
My lack of confidence and esteem just pushes me deeper into self-pitying.
How do I change this?

I'm happy- but unhappy
I'm happy to be alive and well
And breathing
I'm not lonely because I have Lex, Mom, and You
I'm lonely because I have no presence of that I seek
I'm loved because I'm shown with every breath, gift, and hug from my child
I'm unloved because it feels no one else loves me
I wonder if I even love myself

I want to change. I want to metamorphose into what I see inside myself. Only I can do it.
No one understands my point on the issues of "self-conflict". But I do.
I'm struggling to become all I feel I want to be and can be.
I don't know what my issues are some days, others it's like a cloud of smoke: paranoia from a lot of stuff.... like I'm fighting my demons. Divine Creator-
It must be You to keep a sistah moving and grooving.
But most days I feel like I breezed through and never actually lived
What a sucky feeling!

You've protected so many of us and you continue to.

I know you've stepped in on a lot of things that were seen and unseen in people life
That's why I believe in You.
I'm learning and willing to embrace the fact that it's just not my time for love.
If only others could understand it in their lives and not try to MAKE love happen.
I still hold in my heart that you've had grace and mercy on my life and that's why I have his time in my life to reflect, grieve, and find understanding and forgiveness in myself.
But when it comes to love, I've realized that I HAVE TO BE PATIENT.
If only others could understand that in their lives and not try MAKE love happen.
My life has flashed before my eyes so many times; I will not play out for love, affection, acceptance, boredom, loneliness, or stress. It's not a very easy game. Because when you think you're winning- you're losing. But you get just enough satisfaction to keep playing
And eventually, you'll lose again if you don't realize it wasn't your game of love to play.

It's so depressing looking back...The love and lust in me, pulling me down but I've realized that the stress, pressure, and heartache is greater than me and I can wait, I just hope it's not too late.

The devastation at what could've been still hurts....
He charmed me, manipulated me, and was conniving, vindictive- a class act.
Divine Creator- you know I was fine
I was outright fine with being a bitch. But even through them notes, he drew me to him.
When I talked to him, his voice drew me deeper, when I saw him that was it.
I continued to play my role as he continued to play his.
But he was smarter, and well aware that I was all show.

I guess seeing him as never wanting to have sex with me, made me want to give myself to him. He made me want to show my heart, and feel and express what I was holding inside. Even when I wondered if he was seeing someone else, there was this aura about him that led me to believe he was love- different.
I was ready to be with him. I felt so warm and un-alone and unfearful. I had a couple others: looking, picking, and preying on me. And I got nowhere. I realized that it was not my time. If only others could understand it in their lives and not try to MAKE love happen.

Why am I still here? For my baby; who I love so much and want to be closer to and be the one to do her 16th birthday and watch her grow up and be there to see her married and raise my grand babies. Am I here to be there for her through the life pressures she'll be experiencing sooner than later?

I'm having a hard time trying to become the mother I feel inside I am while others dictate my daughter's life and it makes me feel invisible to it all. Making me feel invisible to the point I'm incompetent and don't know what to do to bring her up right.

I want to be able to achieve all of which I'm responsible for, and that's to be a good mom to my baby. I want her to love me as much as I love her and not be angry if I couldn't be or do something she feels a mom should do. But all I can do is try hard and keep a roof over her head, clothes on her, fed, bathed and give her love. Doesn't that count for something?

I've been here before: thinking about life.
Talking, crying, and writing to you.
Wanting life to change and get better.
I know I may be disappointing you at this moment.
Please forgive me, I wanted to just say, "I'm sorry!"
You say, "For What?"
I say, "For being me."
I'm sorry for taking your attempts to save my life for granted by living in vain.
I think and look at myself for who I really am and think why, how... No matter how much I understand things- I really can't get past the has-beens, the shouldn't-haves, the coulda-beens and I'm sorry!
I've been seriously breaking down to the point of abundant grief and strain and pleading. Wanting so bad to go home and be born again- inside and out.
I've talked about reincarnation of the spirit and soul. What about the mind and how it depicts our reality and ways of living and how we handle?
Some people are ruined forever.
Some people never get the chance to see how it would've been because they didn't accept the importance of life and receiving grace and mercy to being saved.
But I have, I really have. And I try to be positive, think well, feel right, be better and do better.
I do.
But I'm afraid.
Humanity has wrapped me up to feel and think otherwise.

I see blessings from you all around me; take them for granted sometimes and focus on what may not be.
I'm sorry for being me.
Everything I feel, see, do, act, and even think sometimes feels like a masquerade.
But I do take a look at the good things when I find the strength to let go of the bad. And I see hope, love, and blessings. I feel Love coming out, but what stops the ongoing transformation?
I feel so weak, so strong, so afraid, so happy, so hopeful, so discouraged, so patient, and so in a hurry. Wanting to fulfill life.
Sometimes I feel like I'm mixed up and confused- wise but unwise- knowing but unknowing.
I want a full, good life but understand that:
Everything is possible and nothing is guaranteed.

I feel like I'm visualizing my life but disillusioned by what I would like to have.
I'm sorry for my mixed feelings.
I'm just afraid of life; afraid of trying to live.
I'm having peace but no peace.
Scared but not.
Fearing life, fearing death, fearing what's in between.
Stuck in my own way- wanting new ways.
I'm sorry for making You sad and angry and mad and disappointed.
I'm sorry for making you cry.
I really wanna make it up to You.
I know my existence is a blessing to myself, my children, and the world.
I gotta make it up to you.
I'm sorry I let you down.
Sorry like I've never been before.

I love you!
But please don't let me get evicted- AGAIN!
I can forget about a house, condo, or another apartment if this happens.
I think I would die of shame and embarrassment if I have to live with another person again. Alexsus is counting on me to keep it together. I've been needing a better job forever but have to admit it's my fault that money has been tight sometimes: from buying things not needed, not wanting to go to work, being late for work, making excuses, hating my job. Not even extremely looking for a job.
It's all my fault.
I haven't been doing enough- period- to handle stuff.

I have to admit I'm ashamed of my idiotic actions like: buying bullshit, and having fun.
I can't afford any of it!
Now rent is late, Christmas is near and gifts are non-existent- and all this could've been avoided if I acted like I had sense.

But it's hard
I feel like I've been given a green light to proceed with life, but it's hard trying to do things "all new"; it's starting to feel like a landslide, and I'm the only one to climb back up and hold down the fort.
I'm tired of all this being late, having crappy jobs, and feeling unable to support me and my child.
I don't want it to be this way anymore- I want everything to be All Good.

―――――

I know that who I am and where I am, I couldn't compare with most....But I don't know how to love myself. I was never really taught... so please teach me. It's only fair. I deserve to be and feel the love for me as other people feel for themselves
So how do I get myself to love? I know I want to do these things to feel good about myself and what I know will be approving to myself:
* Lose 100 pounds... why... because I've never been a normal weight. It's a burden on my health, my image, relationships, and self-love.
* Fix my hair, nails, feet, and teeth... why... because I deserve and need to be maintained. My style and image has fluctuated and is now at a screeching halt when looking in the mirror and loving what I see.
* I want my personality to flourish... why... because I want to be sharp, social, and feel assured about who I am and what I could bring to the table, to the world, my family, and everyone else so that I feel loved and supported.
* I want to begin to express the talents that I know are true to me and would love to share. It feels important because my confidence is shattered- but the love I have in my gifts makes me feel I'm "great".
* I want to fall in love with a man and no matter who or how I am- he loves, likes, respects and adores me for me.
* I want another child. I love her or him already, although I haven't met the daddy yet, but I will... One day he or she will exist.
* Lastly, I want to put aside all the differences, misunderstandings, and complications between the people I love.

―――――

I pray that you'll love and accept me for who I am and the change I'm willing to make in order to be better and live better. I know the gifts of life and living you've given to me are priceless. And I want to honor that.

Thank You So Much! For my new job! I love you, love you, love you. I knew you would come through for me. I never gave up on either of us. I'm so excited about it, and there is nothing I'm willing to do to screw this up. I owe my promptness, efforts, and tolerance to you! I won't do anything that will affect my survival and independence. I'm a grown woman now, which mean the things I've been doing for the last years are inexcusable. I know I have these two months to prove myself, mainly to you and Lex- and the temp agency- that I'm capable of growth and advancement.
I know I have my writing to look forward to; a car; and relocation eventually. Right now, I know, I can do what it takes to make it. I'm feeling better about myself, acting better, thinking better... even eating better. I feel so good. Really good. I just can't describe it. But Thank You. I hope I meet great people and am social, friendly, and respectful- getting that in return. I pray that I understand my duties and am well instructed to do so. I pray I don't complain, but am grateful for the opportunity to once again stand on my own. I love you, thank you.

Here I am again... wanting love and attention from a man when I can get it right in the next room from my child. Will I ever get rid of this feeling? Or will I always be so needy?

I'm tired, lonely, and wanting companionship. Afraid to be alone. In the dark. Fearing death and danger as I have many nights before. I really miss Alexsus right now, just as much as she misses me.
I'm alone- again.
Wanting to be in the light. Comforted with the blanket of God, keeping me safe from all demons and intruders. Allowing me to heal.

I'm holding on to my patience, holding in my attitude, holding back my tongue, and holding on to my dreams. I can't say that I'm not grateful, blessed beyond belief, or deserving, even. I just hate when I come across ignorant to things or don't use common sense and have people see my demonstration of having no knowledge of something.
I hate it.

I hate when I'm exposed for the young and/or old me that I'm trying not to be. I'm so close to retreating into my bubble like I've been, but that's just putting me back at one.

I'm going to go ahead and make note of this...
I think I'm pushing towards termination at my job. It's something I feel, but am not sure of. They probably don't think I'm the same person that started, but I am. I've been under pressure and been intimidated and foolish since the beginning of the year, that I know I'm in limbo. I don't think it's my work so much as my feeling of displacement and becoming standoffish. I get tense, nasty, and bitchy when I'm under pressure. I get hot and cold, bothered and yet unbothered; all these things that are making them second-guess their decision about me. Damn!

I only want what you want for me. I may complain because I don't understand or see the reason in how things are and pray that you can forgive me. I'm still the person you've been molding. But there are things I'm not ready to let go of, and things that just make sense to let go of. I've got to move forward and believe and excel. Grab ahold of what I want and what's meant for me.
I trust that you will continue to guide me through these new challenges and endeavors that are upon me. I pray that you keep me in your security and comfort me when in doubt.
If I can't promote myself for the woman - aka- April Love I'm becoming... who will? If I can't live inside the blessings you give me, how can I appreciate what you've given? So, please forgive me- love me- and hold on to me with all your heart. I need you most right now. I need you to teach me how to love me, soar, and fly above myself.

*To everyone reading, I hope these thoughts, letters and prayers will touch your heart, open your mind, and awaken your spirit. It's my heart's desire to see people transcend... and become the love they truly need.

It's hot in here. I feel like sooner or later I'm going to melt and my body will be submerged under the pressure, yet I'm subdued by my will to be here.
I think a lot about leaving but haven't a clue where to go. I feel like I'm stuck as a non-existent- but my breathing, hearing, seeing and feeling proves me wrong.

Am I hot because the sun is breaking through the night and I'm feeling its light coming through within my soul, awakening my spirit- raising me up? If so... what could be keeping me down?

I've tend to sit and eat here- just like at home.
Damn am I really that miserable again?
Eat because there is nothing to do or nothing exciting enough to do?
See that's the way it is.
I've drank soda, eaten popcorn, and munched all day long since I've gotten here.
Is it that I need more discipline or is it that this is just a part of who I am?

Friends? Me? What friends?
Never had a true friend in my life.
I always wanted a group of friends to call my own.
All the groups I've been a part of weren't a group but merely a chosen few that wreaked chaos and got me in deep shit.
The troubled ones always seems to come for me, the ones I need never do.

What's inside of me needs a lil kick, so to speak- but deep in my soul I know I need to fuse out in the house of God. What keeps me from there I don't know. I'll figure it out. But it's rather funny I ask the Divine Creator to guide me and help me; show me the way yet I still rack my brain trying to figure out my destiny.
Patience. That's it. I remember someone said that worrying will be the death of me.

It hit me today while talking to my boss, that I felt intimidated by anyone that seems smarter than me, more expressive than me. And when anxiety sets in, I get pissed and lose all control other than fighting my way through with communication to the world outside of mine. I guess I don't talk because not of what I'll say- but how I'll say it.
And it's funny because someone said that I intimidated others

---

I began to wonder how and why I'm such a loner.
What personality or psychological incapability I own that keeps me away from others.
I see at least 10-12 people in a group talking, laughing, taking pictures, and enjoying each other. I've never belonged to something such as that.
And don't understand why.
I don't think I know 10 people I consistently talk to.
I'm almost hopeless when it comes to association, communication, and just out right being a people-person like I scream inside to be.

I don't know how I'm going to replace these distractions and worries and emotions and needs and all the other things that take my attention away from me to establishing some kind of mental, physical, emotional stability.
I don't know.
I'm wondering if there's a true reason why I smoke weed.
Is it because I'm a deep thinker, or because I write at best when I'm high, or is it I'm trying to shut out the stresses?

And maybe because I want a broader mind and a bigger plan for my life. And it hurts me to think I might not be able to apply myself and life appropriately and be saved from the torture within.

I literally have to tell myself 'shut up' when I hear the thoughts that goes against who I'm becoming. I'm trying to control all ways of thinking- but I'm in the living, which means I have to decide and choose what I'm willing to sacrifice so to be strong and go for that of: Total. Unconditional. Love. Of Self.

The Divine Creator. I've prayed and cried and poured my heart, soul, and being and surely know is my rescuer and savior, protector and healer.

I can recall a time I felt I didn't believe.
It was a time I was stuck within myself and said I hated and didn't believe.
My soul was in agony.
And knew what I needed most of all was somebody to love me for me and would accept me and welcome me and not use me.
But gaining some control of my emotional-self has gotten me through a lot but left me completely alone
That's the way it needs to be.
Be as I have no control over love.
But I've received bittersweet experiences...
And foreseen possibilities to believe in.
Have opened my eyes, through my mind- although I'm in doubt.
But have been given piece by piece of myself- little by little-
To forgive myself and gain a true heart which establish the grounds for a good soul.

Life is funny like that... No matter how it seems like I'll fail- that voice of recognition, love, perseverance, and belief comes into my mind and overflows my heart that I will get through, and the goodness of my heart will not be in vain- for the spirit of the Creator dwells there and will cast out all the unwanted and unneeded.

I believe in You Divine Creator.
I believe you love Me and want Me to be happy and loved.
I believe I've been kept and chosen.
I believe I will be great- inside and out.
I believe I am healed and made new.
I believe I'm in favor of your grace and mercy.
I believe my life will be good and have value.
I believe I am one with You

It overflowed me with joy that I could provide this guy in need with a little change- with a little piece of myself. It makes me wonder if my folks feel the same as when they lend a hand to me- even though I hold enough pride to abort the fact that I'm blessed.

But just the look in his eyes and smile on his face and the gratefulness in his voice, it showed me that a true sense of humanity lives in us- even me.

My body, style, attitude, personality, and flair all have potential to excel at the highest degree. I'm a rose in bloom and just starting to open up. My baby gurl is still a bud but I'll show her how to bloom in full.

Thank you Divine Creator for being able to walk, talk, feel, hear, see, smile, laugh, write, work, understand, give, love, help, and simplify my life with words of endearment to my soul.
You are awesome and one day I'll come back to you.

As for love... fuck it- I can't make it all go the way I want.
I just gotta do everything else to feel me up and let love, the house on the beach, early retirement, and old age happen when it happens.

These are some questions from the past

Why?
Why was I left alone to conquer things with no knowledge?
Why was it that I had no father, male role model, masculinity?
Why Me?
Where was it when I got taken- my soul- that is? Was I aware?
Is it true that when he molested me and took away my innocence and made me strive for the pleasurable unknown- was that when I acquired lust?
Does this scorpion on my arm mean venom, poison, hurt, pain, hate? Is Deveyes the captive form of letters that produced what the scorpion has?
Am I free? Free of the past, free of the constant knowledge of being lost in darkness? Free of the beautiful masks of the devil: mocking, manipulating, imitating love when all along it's been a charade- a weapon to cast me further from the light of truth?

Am I free of disease, illness, sickness, infection, the inability to live as free as a bird?
Free of hate, hurt, and heartache?
Free of pain, pressure, disloyalty?
Free of being alone, unthought-of, unloved?

God- why, when, will, where, can, is, how am, should, would, could, are, may

---

There's something about outside and the different noises that you hear when you're sitting in silence- waiting for you next move. It's almost relaxing: the still air, the hum of cars, people, insects, and sometimes the TV's that sound.
But in the night, there is a stillness that allows you to relax and calm. Outside, when all is sound inside and asleep, I'm able to free my mind with no distractions and write until my mind is clear.

Why does it feel like I can't take the next step to achieve, or what is holding me back from achieving? Where is my want and yearn for life?

No matter where you came from, how you look, or what you did you have the ability to do and be something great.
So I know every letter I receive back from these agents and publishers won't be an acceptance letter, and all won't be rejection.
Like my mom said: there will be at least one that's going to feel the way I do about my book.
So I have to believe that no matter will become the author I was destined to be.

I'm not at all certain what's wrong with me, but I know what I want to do, and I remember the visions I've had of myself. The hard part is the suffering and sacrifice of morphing into this woman and having her be who I've always wanted and needed her to be: Love

---

Yes, I have to think measurable- make smaller goals... but get sidetracked by life.
What does it take, though? To not let life deter you from your goals?

I've realized that I can't be alone forever, or the type of parent I am, or the type of employee or relative I am. I can't stay single or needy, or overweight. I can't keep dreaming of the life I want to give me and Alexsus. I can't keep wanting and needing and yearning and crying over myself, mistakes, and failures- and even the past. I can't keep seeing men that I want and know I can't, shouldn't, or really don't want to have. I can't keep sleeping late and not getting up to work out or telling Alexsus we're going to do something- and don't.
Not anymore!
This is all going to end, and my life will begin.

I've been stressing about my life.
But thinking about all the lives that are gone or ruined forever and the happenings throughout the world, it has lead me to believe that my life is grand and it could be worst. But right now the Creator is allowing me to live and be with the ones I love; and that's enough to sit down and write and make this decision. A decision about how I plan to change the things I'm stressed about and make room to love myself.

I've thought and stressed about these things at some time or another:

Family, Mistakes Made, My Confidence, Acceptance, Patience, Work, Weight
Men, Friends, Money, Finances, Bills, Responsibilities, Blessings, Love, Health, Moving On, Letting Go, Helping others and Myself, Stress, Loneliness, Bullshit, Heartache and Heartbreak, The Past, Present, Future, Dreams, Goals, Desires, and Self... just to name a few.

So I've decided to outline some solutions, answers, probable reasons, remedies, etc. for each one to help me understand myself and my life better; to become more loving and understanding of myself. I know it will take time, but if I focus on healing and loving myself, maybe this can help me regain a healthier mind, heart, and spirit.

I've decided I won't let life kill me and take away my spirit for living.
The Creator has allowed me to remain and my heart has the desire of all that is good. Fuck what the world has me feeling like- problems come and go, and I feel determined to get past the stress and feelings I've had all my life.
I know there's someone inside me someone who needs to show face, someone who will show the me I need to be.
I'm tired and I'm ready to do something:
Work it, move it, push it, shove it- whatever it takes.

As long as I believe what has been provided and instilled in me is to use to my advantage, how could I let it go to waste and let the world win?

My decision to live beyond the madness of everyday life is clearer than ever. I'm going to take record of my daily stresses and concerns and provide resolutions in how I've handled them.
I'll call it "My Daily Relief".
I'm tired of the same ole feelings, thoughts, negativities, questions, concerns, people, places, things, which has had me underneath myself.
The Creator wants more, and I'm willing to fight for the relevance of what's in store for me that I realize I have to work to witness.

I've decided...
To not be so selfish and self-absorbed or blaming of others: I'm a grown ass woman, who has her own mind, her own bills, her own life- And responsibilities
I will, can, and am in control
I'm the is the director and star in this life
My vision is my destiny
My dreams, goals, and visions won't cease as long as I remain in the light...

I've decided...
No more games, lies, self-destruction.
No more heartbreak that shouldn't and didn't have to be.
No more bullshit from the lips of creeps.
No more free ass, no more on bended knees.
No more following, for I am in the lead.
No more worries, pain, or distress.
No more worrying about what's left for the universe to handle of the mess.
No more crying, no more tear stains.
No more staring at a soul deprived of love without restraint.

I've decided to Live

The Mystery of Me

Where do I start, or have I began, the quest of finding out my truth?

The truth in me, of who I am, is, and will be, is going to take forever long or stay a mystery.

How do I find out?
Where do I go?

Is it possible? Or am I too old?
I guess not.
Learning is a never-ending function. Nothing in life will stop that process.
So am I really just a kid learning and developing my mentality?
The recognition of who April is- I find myself trying to figure me out like others.
A mystery that is Me?

Will you allow me, God, to achieve life? Put the pieces together, to solve this?
I'm ready to be set free and get on with it.
Solving the puzzle, looking for clues, asking witnesses, interrogating criminals, finding the piece of info that will construct and highlight the significance of myself.
To solve the mystery of Me

Right now I want to cry
Cry because I hate my job
Cry because I want to be a better mom
Cry because I want to be with "love"
Cry because I need money
Cry because I have to work
Cry because I'm fat
Just cry, cry, cry
And if I was high- I wouldn't feel the need to cry.
I would just feel as if nothing bothers me.
I'll feel better about what I already know is true.
But I'm not high
I can't be high all the time
I just gotta deal with my shit.

Moisture fading off the leaves, making them dry; sunlight so forceful-bright as if looking at a 5 million watt bulb; shining it's brightness beyond.
I heard it would be fire when judgment day arrives.
Will the power and poison of knowledge consume another human race?
After earth is dust yet again, Man living in a fiery existence, in which we inflict.
As I know now- knowledge has been disastrous in this place.
God will save only a few while others perish.
The sun is so hot, more every year.
Winter & Fall & Spring has disappeared

No more caterpillars, locust, moths
Dragonflies, baby bumblebees
Or fresh grass and green trees
I wonder will rain ever fall like it once had, or the snow will ever fall and light the blackest night.
Days and nights, coldness to cleanse the air, to cleanse the spirits to freeze the fire in our souls.
I wonder will innocence ever be rehabbed.
Will children live to see a childhood I had.
To know who/what the Creator is, to see the light.
To be free from abductors, abusers, traffickers, pedophiles, and absent lost souls, like the face of everyday life.
Will there ever be peace, respect, and helping hands?
Will there ever not be disease and illness in the body and soul of man?
The questions go on and on

My career. A career.
That always sounds good to my ears.
I was born to write and love and set examples.
My mission, I truly believe, is to work to have all I and Alexsus deserves.
I can make this work out for us.
My mission is also to live in a house.
If I write, get my name out there, be who I feel I am, know I am- it just takes time.
The people I'm planning on interacting with
I can have a house.
I'm a living, walking, talking, writing, Victory.
We all are.

I think, well partly sure, I've made a decision on what I'm going to do with myself.
It's hard to change.
Especially when it's more comfortable to keep things the way they are.
If I die today what will I say to the Creator to make me stay?

I'd say "I'm a stupid sinner- in need of love. Please help me to change, so I won't die at a young age- I have a daughter to think of."

I say it's hard because we get used to the settling and not striving for higher, thinking different.
But I know... I do all the time.

My mind can't stay off becoming a bigger and better person- at all.
But I don't even know the feeling I'm looking for I smoke; I don't even know what it is.
But there is a feeling: a dazed- yet insightful- feeling that overcomes.
You're stuck in your fantasies
So I guess I'm scared that if I come down- will the fantasies ever be?

In reality, I know I'm an achieving goal, but when I'm high- it's like seeing where they can go, what they can be.
When I'm grounded- it's a whole other thing.
Life seems harder and stressful.
So I go up into the clouds of bud again, trying to find the truth in something that is not yet seen or will ever be
Up into my fantasies.

I ask myself often, why did I have to be me? Why did everything, and I mean everything, happen and be apart of me?
It's funny, if I'm blessed with a new life and a new me then why is it hard for me to move on? You know I want to so bad that it hurt. I can never forget the past, but the negatives of it always facing me. Everywhere I go. Every person I see.
How the hell do I handle this?
What do I do to move on?

Aroma therapy:
Something to lift your senses.

My favorite- the purple one- is called "Share"
Share in more ways than one.
Share my time and space with Alexsus.
Share my heart with the "the one".
Share my passion of the written word with the world.
Share my love and light with those in need
Purple is my favorite color. My passion for the ups, downs, and experiences in my life, and the power to share.

Next it would be- yellow- it's called "Celebrate"
Celebrate life, and a new beginning.
Celebrate a successful relationship with my daughter.
Celebrate the budding of my career.
Celebrate the blossoming of something true with "him".

Celebrate conquering 25 years of myself to be able to get through to the other side.

Next, there's the green one- "Explore"
Explore life, the world, the possibilities of what out there for me to grab, the opportunities to be more than who I am.
Greater than who I am right now
Explore education, good health, marriage, a business, a career, family, love.
Explore life and grip it with all my might and enjoy the ride on solid-green-ground.

Lastly, the blue one, "Unwind"
You know how I feel about blue
I think water and clear skies.
Refreshing and invigorating
Like fresh mint
I think about the grain of sand under my feet at the shoreline.
The whisper of the wind, cool and soothing
No need for Nyquil near the water.
Just sit and hear the wave roar out in the night and unwind.

Share- the day
Celebrate- the day
Explore- the day
Unwind- at the end of the day

Live.

I try to understand the mentality of the black woman; the unspoken thoughts that produce an attitude so elusive. What makes the sight of eyes saying, 'Who she think she is?' 'Stuck-up bitch-' I don't know where this came from; in the past it was sistahood and together we fought our way through. Now we put each other down profoundly. So messed up. Take your man and fuck with his brother or friends, too. Playing both sides of the field: gay and straight. Who are we for real? But yet think they are the shit. All the while with a conniving smile, the presence of a woman too proud- in a cloud so dark we can't see... Sistahs we need to stick together, respect ourselves and each other, and that way we can set our minds free. And get control of these black men who are disrespecting us and neglecting their responsibilities.

I've made it to "25"! I feel like my life has to start to change. No more holding back or holding on. I have to see the next 25 years through. And there isn't any more time to waste. Everything from my spirit, to my body, to my bank accounts have to flourish and be in abundance.
I know it's in me to do. I woke me up with a purpose; I'm telling the truth when I say I have no thought or emotions today. It's as if I breezed right through. My conscious was as clear and unstained as I can remember in a while. Funny how all my negative thoughts have been shifting. But I know that I can't have life or myself being in the way it's been. I really, truly, have too much passion, insight, and talent to be in the position I'm in. I'm going to finally control myself and see what happens to me because I have the spirit to go for the gold of my goals.
It's in me to achieve... Love is in me to win.
I've been so scared of not living and failure; not seeing I was enough or worthy enough. I've thought terrible things about myself. As well as done. I deserve the chance to feel differently about it all...
Especially myself... I want love ssooooooooo BAD in my life. I've come to realize that I gotta love me and love living just the same as I want it returned.
I didn't get many calls today- not even my daughter.
I love her. Right now I feel so unattached to her, but in my soul I know we're still connected. I need to feed off her existence 'Cause she needs me more than I've ever needed anyone.

Deep inside of my heart is where I feel most vulnerable when it comes to love. I feel threatened with my emotions sailing through the pit of my being... allowing me to feel again what I want and what's been missing so far throughout my life.
that love that is needed throughout a lifetime and lives to come; that love that fills me with joy as it once had when I was a child- fearless to the terrible unknown of reality.
That love that had comforted me in the womb of my mother, my daughters hugs and in the arms of my lover... that love that never really left and came back and always remained a part of me...
The love for me...

All the time I spent with myself, I'd never understood how and why I'd let those feeling of boredom, loneliness, abandonment and my emotions I didn't know of take me to the next activity there was to do when there was nothing else to do... EAT!

Most- if not all- of my life I've figured things out on my own. Just jumped out there and tried. I guess that sums up a lot of my experiences. Trying to figure out what I could do, where I belonged, what I should say. What will make this happen or that. Questions that I had no formal knowledge of anyone's teachings because everyone seemed so focused on themselves. Thank goodness I had me.
Failing myself, Lex, fam, job, health, life, is forever a worry for me. I just want something to be not necessarily easy, but just not a struggle to keep order. I want to know and not figure. I feel like I can and should be a lot more and better than where I stand in life right now. It's ironic to feel this way and want so badly, but don't know how to master a way to get to the point of comfort. I want to be something great and leave something behind that my kids and grandkids could see and be proud of. I just... I don't know. See, I say that too often. Is there anything that I'm sure about anymore? I'm listening to myself and hearing this woman that is pleading and crying like a frightened little girl... about life.

Love
You know, I wonder how do people who never had someone to love and love them back go on.
Do they pretend that someone is there, are they content that this is how their lives are set?
Are they miserable in the mind, heart and spirit?
I wonder if they've lost faith or just accepted that it's that way.
I can't even imagine

Who is "He"?
Where is "He"?
When will "He"- come into my life and give his heart to me?

When I was trying to come to grips with my reality at one point, I felt that it was no other way than to go to church; I had no other options left for myself.
That's when I gave my life to Christ. Although I was afraid to make it official with a baptism, I knew what was really on my mind, more than anything... Living.
I've been in some earthly hell to the point that a few time I rather been in real Hell. But the God in me has talked, guided, and allowed me to live

through this life so I can know the truth about myself and free my heart and soul.

At most, all I can do is gain and achieve what it is I want. I'm no longer a "hater". I may be a little intimidated by other woman's success, but I've learned to accept the things I have in my life NOW and focus on what I want to accomplish.

It's a wonderful thing to have to do what I do- I can actually see and feel myself progress in steps. It's clear that I have to get grounded and take the first step in obtaining one goal. Because anything good to come is worth being patient with myself.

I've just completed reading the book "Value in the Valley" by Iyanla Vanzant. There are a lot of things in there I want to highlight and a lot that I need to reread to absorb. It's a really powerful book- in terms of your spirit and its ability to strengthen you when life is driving you madd.

I believe "A Rose is Still a Rose is going to do better than people expect because it touches on the spirit and its conflict with the heart, mind, and emotions. Women are going to relate to the characters in the book in some way or another. I believe it will be a bestseller! It will. I know it will; I can feel it. Because it is "real". It is women- today- in life. I can only hope the sequel reinforces the belief in love and belief in myself to produce a novel that defines "true" women.

Today I said good things about my body and acknowledged it for all it does for me. I went from my feet to my head and described the positivity that it acquires that I live by.

I've never done anything like that- ever. And it brought me a sense of joy and happiness that I've never experienced when it comes to my body. Then I was to put an image in my mind of what my body should be like, and I am pleased.

I'm here thinking of all the efforts I'm consciously making to change my life. The fact that I've been aware and am now taking control and responsibility make me feel a lot stronger in the decision I'll be facing soon-to-come. I'm not going to attest that I'll be perfectly fit to handle all the challenges now, but I am willing to give my all to a situation. As of now, I am just trying to get a feel for my conscience and my ability to do the things I feel I can and want to do. The efforts are necessary. The positive affirmations are necessary, and the focus to do all these things are necessary. Reading, Writing, Meditating, Praying- helps me to become better and better.

On the man front, right now, I need to be single and not date until I'm happy with myself and content with my life. Peace will lead me to that contentment, but doing and changing and loving myself in ways that's good for me is what I need to show in my mate. Not a woman who doesn't look at herself in the mirror, or feels bad about herself. I want him to see the power I have over myself and my life- not look at me now and see that I am distressed and in pain. Although I'm not a burden... why be with someone who is unhappy with themselves?

I'm finding it to be the most challenging thing; understanding my emotions to actually give up what I thought fulfilled me seems so easy than changing for the role you're suppose and want to take in life. I swear my position in this world will be great. As I unmask and peel the layers of myself to be my greatest self and achieve my highest aspirations, I plan to lay down work of a magnitude to hopefully change a group of people that can affect the change of the world. For I know I am a person that can make things possible

---

I know that this overwhelming joy can only come in the ways of me setting my mind and heart and body up for the loves of my life- be that career, relationships, foundational growth, and a more secure closeness with my child I've only imagined.
Right now I'm growing in myself. This is what I want. No more am I the 6-year-old, 8-year-old, 11-year-old, 13-year-old, 15-year-old, or the 19-year-old, 21-year-old, or the 25-year old that has perished in her belief of an unconventional love. But as I am times after, is a woman that believes in herself as worthy and deserving of the true, real love. The love that only she can have in herself to manifest the love she will live by and survive on in her life. I am so happy that I am able to start anew.

I know I have a long way to go, but I've never been so ready in my life to ride the wave to freedom. It's a rush... a natural feeling of self-worth and knowledge of what I need to make me want to live and why.

Men are no longer my love source- I am and my child is. Food is no longer my stimulant and filler of needs- love is... and the devil with its lost, wandering spirits is no longer holding me in the dark... the Divine Creator is my Source of Light and Love, and together we will lead me to the transcendence of myself.

For I am coming out of the Valley...

Into Life.

Transcending.

Favorite Quotes and Sayings

Love has the innate ability to look past the human and into the godly*- Colette Burnham

#1 is to be an individual, cloning yourself to be like others is grounds for defeat- April Love

"I will change on the inside which will reflect outside- but I realize I got to get the inside right before I can ever truly allow anyone to love me the way I want, need, or deserve"

Common sense and logic is the key to making life not so complicating- April Love

Never take your child's life for granted; the history of you is never known, unless you raise your child to flourish with love and gratitude - April Love

A hearts needs and desires are always going to conflict with emotions- April Love

No one but ME is all about me- April Love

No matter where you came from, how you look, or what you did you have the ability to do and be something great- April Love

God has given me too many gifts, chances and love to throw it all away on the fear of meeting my potential and living out the true me- April Love

Obstacles are those frightful things you see when you take your eyes off the goal- Henry Ford

Go out into the world today and love the people you meet. Let your presence light new light in the hearts of people- Mother Teresa

Success consists of getting up just one more time than you fall- Oliver Goldsmith

The deeper that sorrow carves into your being, the more joy you can contain- Kahlil Gibran

You should not suffer the past. You should be able to wear it like a loose garment, take it off and let it drop- Eva Jessye

Courage is being scared to death- and saddling up anyway- John Wayne

The supreme happiness of life is the conviction of being loved for yourself, or, more correctly, being loved in spite of yourself- Victor Hugo

"For centuries, purple has been the symbol for royalty..." (my fave color 🙂)

People may fall many times but they become failures only when they being to blame someone else- Unknown

It was never what I wanted to buy that held my heart's hope. It was what I wanted to be- Lois McMaster Bujold

The curious paradox is that when I accept myself just as I am, then I can change- Carl Rogers

Though no one can go back and make a brand new start, anyone can start from now and make a brand new ending- Carl Bard

Don't let life discourage you; everyone who got where he is had to begin where he was- Richard L. Evans

Education is when you read the fine print. Experience is what you get if you don't.

Thoughts have power. Thoughts are energy. And you can make your world or break your world by your thinking- Susan L. Taylor

"Positive thoughts can make a difference in your life. Despair and depression shut you down, whereas positive thoughts keep hope in action. Can you allow positive thoughts to lift you?"

Get a life in which you are not alone. Find people you love, and who love you. And remember that love is not leisure, it is work- Anna Quindlen

To be blind is bad, but worse is to have eyes and not see- Helen Keller

Sometimes the seeds of happiness are sown in darkness- Unknown

Some people succeed because they are destined to, but most people succeed because they are determined to- Unknown

Hate is like acid. It can damage the vessel in which it is stored as well as destroy the object on which it is poured- Ann Landers

You have the capacity to choose what you think about. If you choose to think about past hurts, you will continue to feel bad. While it's true you can't change the effect of the past influences had on you once, you can change the effect they have on you now- Gary McKay, Ph.D.

Have patience with all things but first with yourself. Never confuse your mistakes with your value as a human being. You're a perfectly valuable, creative worthwhile person simply because you exist. And no amount of triumphs or tribulations can ever change that. Unconditional self-acceptance is the core of a peaceful mind- St. Francis de Sales

"You can't base your life on other people's expectations."

"An open mind collect more riches than an open purse."

Worrying is like a rocking chair: it gives you something to do, but it doesn't get you anywhere- Unknown

Wisdom is the ability to do good and to abandon sin- Gerondi

It takes as much stress to be a success as it does to be a failure- Emilio James Trujillo

It is not our abilities that show what we truly are. It is our choices- Professor Dumbledor (Harry Potter- Chamber of Secrets)

I can be changed by what happens to me. But I refuse to be reduced by it- Maya Angelou

While everything is changing, you are changing, too. Trust your new self to adapt in all things you do- Maya Angelou

I'd rather be a failure at something I enjoy than being a success at something I hate- George Burns

Be not afraid of growing slowly, be afraid only of standing still- Chinese proverb
Just when you are reduced materially, take care not to be impoverished also spiritually- J. Kimhi

Prayer does half, repentance does all- Levi, Leviticus Rabb

Be the love that you are looking for and it will come back around to you- Line in a Horoscope

Never go to a doctor whose office plants have died- Erma Bombeck

He who loves brings God and the World together- Buber

A strong positive mental attitude will create more miracles than any wonder drug- Patricia Neal

The greatest mistake in life is to be continually fearing you will make one- Elbert Hubbard

When you touch a fellow human being in love, you are doing God's work. See within each human being a fallen angel- Pat Rodegast and Judith Stanton

Everything is possible and nothing is guaranteed- April Love

Love yourself... it's your daily gift to you- April Love

I believe in love. I believe that with love comes purpose and with purpose comes responsibility, and longevity to sustain that purpose- April Love

My feelings of love is what gets me through myself and through the day. It gives me all that it can bring, and even in my most painful moments, love carries me on- April Love

I always knew I was destined for greatness- Oprah Winfrey

Thank You! Thank You! Thank You! Thank You!

Thank you to all who bought this book. It means a lot to me. It's a pleasure to express myself in the truest form that only the human spirit can relate to.

For whatever this book does for you, I hope you enjoyed it and pray you take away whatever positive it can be used for. I hope you will continue to support me in the years to come and the works to follow. And truly want to thank you for "just reading".

Reading is the gateway to a world known and unknown; imagined and realized; dreamed and ways to make a dream come true.

Love Always,

April

Lessons Learned from Book One

About the Author

April Love is a writer by many definitions. Her main love is the written word in its creative form. She's used this gift in many facets; i.e. writing for businesses, musicians and for private affairs in the realm of: wedding vows, eulogies and love letters. She's recited poetry and spoken word at many events and venues. Most recently she taught a life skills writing class to middle and high school youth.

She remembers how writing helped her face the realities of life while creating a safe space where she can set her heart free and soothe her soul.

Growing up in an entrepreneurial family, she learned how to do many things while assisting her family in the many side hustles and businesses they pursued. Her professional and work life spans many industries and hustles of her own where she ultimately went on to gain various skillsets through areas such as finance and accounting, catering and event planning, administration and small business management. Most before the age of 30.

Using her writing skills to create business, technical and creative content within the likes of Tomorrow's Catering, Inc., Washington Performing Arts Society, US Holocaust Museum, American Correctional Association, Court Service and Offender Supervision Agency, Maryland Department of Human Services and Department of Labor and have went on to work for herself as a cleaning contractor, freelance writer and business consultant.

Thankful for such accomplishments to serve in her local community in fascinating ways, its allowed her the exposure to different worlds and people to set her up for her own success.

This is only the beginning.

Connect with April as she will be adding new content as she expand and promote her self-publishing and business aspirations.

www.ingramcontent.com/pod-product-compliance
Lightning Source LLC
Chambersburg PA
CBHW022105160426
43198CB00008B/355